A C

Notebook

ROBERT FINCH

Robert Finch

Illustrations by Jason Hart

On Cape Publications

Cape Cod, Massachusetts
www.oncapepublications.com

© 2011 Robert Finch

10 9 8 7 6 5 4 3 2 1

All rights reserved. No part of this book may be reprinted without the express written permission of On Cape Publications, Inc. with the exception of brief quotations for book reviews.

All illustrations are by Jason Hart.
Cover/book design and production by Jason Hart. Raspberry Productions
www.raspberryproductions.com
Copyedited by Susan Bouse, Bouse Editorial.
Supervision of design, editing, and production by Adam Gamble.
Front Cover photo by Adam Gamble.
Back Cover photo by Adam Gamble.

ISBN-13: 9780978576691

For further information, write to On Cape Publications, Inc., 41 Janall Drive, Dennis, MA 02638.

Printed in the United States of America.

Contents

Introduction

The following essays are a selection of radio scripts from a weekly program, *A Cape Cod Notebook*, which began airing on WCAI, the Cape and Islands NPR station, in October 2005. In a strange way, these weekly broadcasts represent a coming full circle for me. Few people, I suspect, remember or know (or care) that I began my professional writing career on Cape Cod on a local radio station in 1972. The station was the old WVLC (Voice of the Lower Cape) in Orleans, the first local radio station on the Lower Cape. The programs were all locally produced and featured local amateurs as well as several semiretired announcers and stars from network radio's golden era, including Julie Stevens, who played the lead role in *The Romance of Helen Trent*, the longest-running radio soap opera of all time. (My favorite WVLC program was *Franny Nickerson's Musical Giants*, a Saturday-morning, classical-music show hosted by the eponymous Franny Nickerson. The program featured a major composer each week suggested by a member of the radio staff. For example, "This week Ted Bell's Musical Giant is— Beethoven!")

In those days, I was a young, aspiring, and still-unpublished writer recently returned to Cape Cod, where I hoped to make a career. By day,

I worked as a carpenter, but I also had a part-time job (very part-time) writing publicity notices for the Cape Cod Museum of Natural History in Brewster. At one point, the museum thought it might reach a wider audience through a radio show, and John Hay, then the museum's president, asked me if I would do a museum-sponsored, nature-oriented weekly radio program for WVLC. I had never done any professional radio work; more to the point, I knew virtually no natural history. Still, it seemed a professional opportunity, and the museum had an excellent natural-history library, and so, on April 16, 1973, *Cape Naturalist of the Air* began airing weekly on WVLC.

It was not an illustrious run. In fact, it was embarrassing. For one thing, I had never been coached in radio reading, and my delivery was stiff and uninflected. For another, I was basically like the substitute teacher who tries to stay one lesson ahead of the class. I would pick a topic—birds' nests, say, or the herring run—go to the museum library and cram for several hours, then write up a five-minute script trying to sound (rather unsuccessfully, I'm afraid) as if I knew what I was talking about. The only solace I took was that it wasn't much worse than some of the other programs on the station.

I was helped in recording the programs by Ted Bell, a veteran of network radio who was heroically patient with my inept efforts and who edited the recordings. In those ancient days, of course, recordings were done on reel-to-reel tapes, and I have a vivid memory of Ted emerging from the engineer's booth after one recording session, holding up a thirteen-inch length of recording tape.

"What's that?" I asked.

"A cough."

Despite its failings, *Cape Naturalist of the Air* ran for over two years, at which point John Hay approached me and, in his characteristically gentle way, said, "Uh, Bob, maybe radio isn't your best medium." I wasn't about to put up an argument, but it turned out he had also spoken to his friend Ray Rogers, the editor of the Dennis *Register*. Ray offered to let me write a weekly natural-history column instead. To no one's regret, *Cape Naturalist of the Air* quietly disappeared, and on February 13, 1975, *Soundings*, a weekly museum-sponsored column, began appearing in the *Register* and was eventually printed in four (then–independently owned) Cape Cod weekly papers.

The rest, as they say, is history—at least, my history. *Soundings* ran for eight years and was well-received. A chance visit of a Boston editor to her parents on the Cape led to my first book offer, for *Common Ground*, a collection of *Soundings* columns. Eventually, I outgrew the confines of a newspaper column and began publishing longer pieces in regional and national magazines. Six other books and two anthologies have followed.

It has been a rewarding career, and I feel lucky to have been able to make a living writing about a place I love, but I have always missed the editorial freedom and the immediate local feedback I got while doing the newspaper columns. So, when Jay Allison offered me the opportunity to do a weekly broadcast on WCAI in Woods Hole, I jumped at the chance. Jay had a national reputation as a radio producer, and his innovative blend of national-network and locally produced programming had already changed the radio-listening habits of many people on the Cape and Islands. The first *Cape Cod Notebook* was broadcast on September 20, 2005, a little over three decades after my first radio attempt.

Several things were different this time around. For one thing, I now knew something of what I was talking about. Also, my wife, Kathy Shorr, who has had considerable radio experience here on the Cape, initially coached me in how to read effectively on the radio. I was given *carte blanche* as to subject matter, and although most of the scripts I've done have been "nature oriented," they are much more personal essays than nature essays. As I've tried to indicate, it was more happenstance than choice that I began my writing career as a nature writer. In fact, I have spent the better part of thirty years trying to disown the title of "naturalist." I have no formal natural-history training, although, over the years, I have formed parasitic relationships with genuine field naturalists for my own purposes. Still, I have too much respect for their profession to appropriate it.

The truth is, I've always been at least as interested in human beings and human nature as I have been in wild animals and the natural world. In fact, I regard my main subject to be the intersection between people and nature—which is one reason why Cape Cod has been such a fertile ground for me. I think of these radio scripts as a more honest reflection of my interests as a writer. You will find here essays on donut shops, beach bonfires, French bakeries, classical music, newspaper deliverers, roadside diners, and national politics cheek-by-jowl with those on shorebirds, weather, scratching for quahogs, hummingbirds, and whales. We do, after all, have a foot in each world in our daily lives.

It's been a great pleasure doing these radio programs over the past six years, and WCAI's listeners have been an active part in these broadcasts. I've appreciated all of the comments and feedback I've received—whether by e-mail, snail mail, or face-to-face—even when, in the minds of a few listeners, I haven't measured up to being the "model" of behavior I never set out to be. I've also been gratified to see how flexible and

5

adaptive NPR audiences can be with a writer doing radio pieces. At the beginning of the show's run, I was cautioned by some of the radio staff to write in a plain style: "short, simple sentences—no subordinate clauses." But as I continued to produce scripts, some of the ideas I wanted to explore required a more complex style, and I've been pleased to find that, by and large, the radio audience has had little trouble with it. Make a topic interesting, I believe, and most listeners will make the effort to follow you.

As a writer, I've also been stimulated by having a weekly deadline again and challenged by a format even more constricting than my original radio show or the old *Soundings* columns. Specifically, because these programs must be slipped in between national NPR "feeds" of *Morning Edition* and *All Things Considered*, I'm strictly limited to six hundred words, or about three-and-one-half to four minutes. (There are a few essays in this collection that are roughly twice the average length. These are where I did the occasional "two parter" on the air, another radio rule the station has let me occasionally break. For the purposes of this collection, I have in these cases combined the two parts into one essay.)

I am grateful to many people for the opportunity to have done these radio broadcasts. First and foremost, my appreciation and admiration go to Jay Allison for his vision and determination in creating such an innovative and stimulating radio station and for making it possible for me to be associated with such a quality enterprise. I owe many thanks to Steve Young, the station's broadcast director during its first decade, who guided me through the initial stages of producing *A Cape Cod Notebook*. It's also been a privilege and a pleasure to meet and get to know the rest of the radio staff and several of the other hosts of locally produced shows, such as Mindy Todd, Vern Laux, and Elspeth Hay. There is a rewarding sense of community between the radio staff of WCAI and its listeners, most evident at the highly popular "Pub Nights" the station sponsors in various local watering holes in the winter.

Over the years, several listeners have asked me to collect and publish a selection of these broadcasts. When I finally began looking around for a suitable publisher, I found the perfect one in Adam Gamble, whose press, On Cape Publications, has been publishing and reprinting quality books about the Cape and Islands for a number of years. Hooking up with Adam for this book has been another serendipitous coming full circle. Years ago, Adam was a student of mine in a course on Cape Cod Literature I gave at the Cape Cod Community College. He was one of my top students, and it was always a pleasure to read and work on his essays. Now, the favor has been returned.

Finally, I want to extend a special thanks to the production engineer and unsung hero of *A Cape Cod Notebook*, Brian Morris. First of all, by being able to record the program at his studio in North Eastham, I've been spared the necessity of weekly drives to Woods Hole. Secondly, Brian's skilled editing has enabled me to sound much more professional on the radio than I am. He has removed numerous coughs (digitally, now, of course) and other vocal errata that I was not even aware of at the time and has woven various retakes seamlessly into the final product. One of the fundamental rules of reading to a radio audience that my wife conveyed to me was, "Read as if you were reading to one person." In this case, that one person is Brian. Seeing him on the other side of the glass panel in the soundproof recording booth, I really do feel I am reading to him; indeed, that somehow I am writing them *for* him.

Plus, he plays a mean guitar.

Robert Finch
Wellfleet, Massachusetts
February 2011

January

Nauset Spit on New Year's Day

Every year, I try to take a walk on New Year's Day on Nauset Beach in Orleans. I began this practice over forty years ago, and it's never lost its novelty or failed to present me with discovery. Every place on Cape Cod and the Islands changes, of course, but Nauset Beach seems to experience change of a higher order than most. This was, in fact, scientifically confirmed a few years ago when studies of the coastline here revealed that the average rate of erosion on Nauset Beach in recent decades has been seven feet per year, nearly twice the average for most other sections of the ocean beach.

This year, I arrived at the beach parking lot on New Year's morning at 6 a.m. It was quite cold, about twenty degrees, clear, and still dark. The lightest of breezes flowed out of the northwest, due to turn northeast and bring in some snow by late afternoon. Offshore, a high bank of smoky clouds delayed the coming of dawn. Three lighted ships moved slowly and smoothly north along the horizon.

The sea was calm and flat gray, a sheet of shimmering metal. The tide was low and rising with small breakers purling and curling in, spreading out from the middle in both directions like the final, quiet, repeated chords of Barber's

"Adagio for Strings." I took a last sip of coffee, pulled up my hood, and got out of the car.

Setting off north toward the inlet to Nauset Harbor, I kept to the inner edge of the dune ridge. My bones were still cold from sleep, but steady movement soon warmed them. The back dunes wore a winter-blasted look; ragged, wiry, gray mops of poverty grass dotted the colorless sand between irregular, brittle mats of lime-green reindeer lichen. The wind scythed through the wheat-colored winter beach grass, stirring dry stands of old cattail reeds in the marsh and setting them to rattling like sabers. Weak yellow light began to seep in from the east. The only bright spots of color on the landscape were the shriveled Chinese-red rose hips, dangling like forgotten Christmas ornaments from the bare, rounded, spiked clumps of beach rose.

Eventually, I came out onto the broad, flat, sandy plain of Nauset Spit, where piping plovers and least terns nest in summer. Now, inexplicably, I began to find the dead bodies of birds, half-covered with wind-driven sand. There were several eiders, a headless cormorant and a headless brant, two large Canada geese, and numerous gulls in their characteristic smashed or slapped-down postures. Many of these bodies looked like they had been worried at by dogs or coyotes.

At first, I kicked up each of these bodies, inspecting them for possible causes of death:

traces of oil, shotgun pellets, emaciation, infection. I was trying to determine whether they had died by some human agency or were just part of nature's great mortality. Eventually though, I stopped examining the stiff forms. The distinction between human and natural death begins to blur and lose significance in such a place. This wide, open, gravelly plain is surely one of the great natural stages of this or any other land. It possesses a kind of submissive power and integrity born of its naked exposure. Here, on the first morning of a new year, among a graveyard of birds serving as their own half-hidden markers, it spoke of bare survival, without benefit of man's flattery, whose only mercy is the driving cover of the wind.

Regional Weather

After our pre-Christmas blizzard last month—the one that dumped up to two feet of snow on the Cape and Islands—I got a call from a friend of mine in Vermont. He was calling, he said archly, to inquire about the "dusting" we'd received. It reminded me that people are still possessive and proud about their regional weather, and nowhere do they harbor these feelings more closely and separately than in the various corners of New England.

For all our talk about a digital, global village where location is increasingly irrelevant, there are still rough natural zones, reasonably distinct areas where the weather determines a part of one's general outlook, consciously or unconsciously.

In this respect, New England is by far the most provincial region of the country. A Vermonter, for instance, is still much more interested in the distinction between his weather and that of the "flatlanders" (as Vermonters delightedly refer to everyone east of the Connecticut River) than he is about California earthquakes or Mississippi floods. And, for that matter, so am I.

It's a matter of identity, I suppose, this playful deriding of the meteorological blandness of one's closer neighbors. My friend's remark, I know, was intended to get a rise out of me, but

I'm not about to quibble with him. I've visited north of Boston enough to know that he's right. Our snow, however deep, doesn't build lasting walls here as it does in Vermont. We experience no real storm fear or the right to emerge looking like survivors in the morning. Our lakes and streams don't disappear under white for months on end. We don't forget the color of the ground, nor do we have starving deer stumbling into our back pastures, even if we had pastures anymore. Here, we have no true "locking time," as they call deep winter up north, and therefore no true "unlocking time."

I would agree with him that our Cape snowstorms are mostly a matter of inconvenience rather than a true threat. Our deepest impression of them is aesthetic, not fearful. We make snowmen that melt even as we build them; we're delighted by snow scenes that we rush to photograph before the afternoon thaw turns them to ugly slush. There's always something ephemeral about the Cape's blizzards. We can't take them with absolute seriousness the way they do in Vermont.

So I'm not about to suggest a comparison on the basis of a foot or two of snow, most of which was gone by the end of the week anyway. Vermont has its snow, and we have our wind. If I want to, I too can play country and chide my friend about his mountain "breezes," or suggest a brisk walk along Race Point in February.

One of the nice things about New England is that you can't generalize about it, or perhaps that's the only generalization. Our weather is too individual, our terrain too densely varied. In fact, it is this stubborn resistance to generalization that helped to spawn that multiplicity of attitudes that makes our cultural history so delightful and regional cooperation so difficult.

Perhaps it was the changeable nature of our weather that taught the old Cape Codders not so much to endure it stonily, like their northern cousins, but to roll with the punches. Perhaps it was the fickle diversity of our weather that developed in them a taste for the unpredictable, a tolerance for the odd, and a skepticism about all forms of permanence.

Rooting for Oysters

I went down to Chipman's Cove yesterday at noon to get some oysters. It was a bright, calm, warm winter's day. There were already a dozen or more cars and trucks parked along the narrow, one-lane dirt track at the end of Cove Road, and, as usual, I had to squeeze my van up against the fence. It pleases me that the only access to the town's main public shellfish beds is a narrow, rutted track with no room to turn around between the bearberry-covered hill on the left and the marsh on the right. The common practice here is for people to leave their keys in their cars so that they can be moved if they're blocking another vehicle.

At the beginning of the season, oystering is more like flower picking. We stroll genteelly out on the flats, selectively picking the fattest shellfish. No more. By this time of the year, the visible oysters are mostly skinny "bananas" in dense clusters, or the occasional large oyster that is encrusted with too many undersized ones to pick off.

Watching some of the commercial shellfishermen who were all around me, I saw that I would have to get down in the thick, black skin of muck that had been brought in by recent storms and *root* around in it, with chisels and gloved hands, to find the buried keepers. Instead of flower pickers, we were now more like pigs going after truffles, getting down on our hands and knees in the thick, oily mud, giving up any pretense to cleanliness to get our treasures into our buckets. I thought of Yeats's Crazy Jane and her assertion that "A woman can be proud and stiff / When on love intent; / But Love has pitched his mansion in / The place of excrement." Yes, love, and oysters, too.

Near me was a young woman with long, blond, straight hair pulled back in a twist. She was talking loudly to another woman as she picked her way across the mud. From her talk and her demeanor, she was obviously a commercial-license holder. She stood, legs straight, orange-booted feet spread wide apart, expertly and efficiently rooting, culling, scraping off the seed oysters, and filling her bag. Her voice was enthusiastic, good-humored, the kind that conveys vitality to the listener. Her talk was mostly of trucks—which were better, Toyotas or Mazdas, and a strange ailment that her truck had, stalling for no reason so that she would have to make an appointment with Charley to put it up on the lift.

She obviously took great joy in her work and the day, but admitted that she was "ready for the ice." "I got my beds tucked in nice and snug," she said, as if she were a kind of housemother to the oysters. She smiled at me when she saw me looking at her. She seemed one of those wonderful people who greet everything, good and bad, with a kind of native enthusiasm.

I don't believe in invidious comparisons, but years ago, when I lived in another town up-Cape and went out on the flats for quahogs, I never heard anyone talk like this. I don't know why this is. Some of it may be because of the different nature of the towns or the relative age of its inhabitants, but mostly, I think, it comes from having a *working* shellfish community here. Men and women working together and apart out here on the flats is what gives their voices such music. All I know is, I could have stayed and listened to her all day.

A Mystery Wrapped in a Conundrum

On the night of January 28, 2008, just south of Newcomb Hollow in Wellfleet, a fierce northeaster pried the ancient hull of a wooden schooner off the ocean bottom and, with incomprehensible force, lifted it intact onto the upper beach. In the weeks following, thousands of off-season visitors came from all over New England, and beyond, to see this latest mystery thrown up by the sea.

The wreck *was* an impressive object. About sixty feet long, it was composed of a series of massive curved six-by-ten-inch oak ribs, with three-inch-thick planking attached to them by means of wooden pegs and iron spikes. Although the hulk must have sat on the sea bottom for close to a hundred years, the wood appeared to be in a perfectly preserved state.

All shipwrecks attract crowds, but one of the things that added to the lure of this particular wreck was the mystery of its identity. Despite its massive size and well-preserved state, there seemed to be no definitive clues to the ship's age or origin. Experts who looked at it offered dates that ranged from the seventeen hundreds to the late nineteenth century. With over three thousand wrecks along this coast over the centuries, there were plenty of candidates for the identity of this one, and several were offered, but no one could say with certainty what ship it was, when it was wrecked, or how long it had lain under the sea.

But beyond the mystery of the ship's origin and identity, the whole scene was wrapped in several conundrums as well. One day, several weeks after it arrived, I visited the wreck again with several dozen other people. A young boy who was there with his father said in wide-eyed wonder, "Do you think it's a Viking ship, Dad?" The grown-ups around him, including me, smiled and chuckled condescendingly at his naïveté. But then, I thought, do we adults really know any more about the ship's identity than the boy did? Oh, we stood around commenting on it, but weren't we really just repeating things we had read or heard somebody else say about it? Could any of us really have said how we knew it *wasn't* a Viking ship?

Another conundrum was the wreck's legal status. There were several small National Park Service signs surrounding the wooden hull, warning visitors that the wreck was, under federal law, a "protected cultural resource" and that it was therefore illegal "to excavate, remove, disturb, deface or destroy" any part of it. Fair enough, I thought, if the National Seashore planned to preserve the wreck for study or to make an exhibit of it. But they didn't. The signs themselves admitted that the wreck would, in time, be reclaimed by the ocean, "to be buried again until the next time the sea uncovers it."

Just a couple of generations ago, any shipwrecks on the beach were fair game for local residents, who saw them as a valuable source of salvage and usable lumber. And there were signs that the old instinct for wrecking was still alive. Despite the warnings, several chunks of the ship's ribs had already been sawn or chipped away, and I heard one man mutter what many must have been thinking: "I wish there weren't so many people around—that peg there looks pretty loose."

And why not? I thought. If the wreck was going to be reclaimed by the sea anyway, why not let us grab some piece of it before it goes, something that will give us some connection, if only in our imaginations, with a more adventurous and earnest past? In our increasingly digital and virtual world, we seem to crave, more than ever, some contact with something so solid, something fashioned by hand from oak beams and iron spikes, something that could last so long at the bottom of the sea and be thrown up, as if in rebuke, to our wondering eyes.

February

A Hard Freeze

When the infrequent hard freeze comes to the Cape and Islands, as it did briefly last month, our land begins to wear a different aspect. It is not quite so fluid, so mobile, so pliant—not quite so open to change by wind and wave. Dunes and beaches stiffen up and present an unaccustomed hard surface to our feet, which now leave no prints. Out of the north, a knife wind drives down the Outer Beach, blowing a scattering of winter dunlins and a few horned larks before it like lost souls.

Cape Cod Bay begins to stiffen at its edges, leaving a salt-ice sculpture of the tide's retreat, complete with ripple marks. Oak leaves, which last month slapped wetly along the soft earth, now do a little frozen jig over iron ground. The tightened branches of blueberry bushes break off at the touch, like crystal. Where the wind has cleared the ground, the saturated earth it- self thrusts up thousands of tiny ice spears, each topped with a tiny clod of frozen dirt. Things tighten up and squeeze out the excess.

Snow and cold push animals and humans into unaccustomed places. One day, a hermit thrush showed up among the chickadees at my feeder. "Some cold," he seemed to say, in ex- planation for his unaccustomed presence. The next day, I spotted a great blue heron on one of Wellfleet's shallow, frozen ponds. He stood alone, on one long leg, out in the middle of the ice, surveying the bleak scene motionlessly with stoic silence. Herons, even in extremity, are not known to come to bird feeders, and when marshes and freshwater shallows freeze over, some die of starvation.

Throughout the unusually warm first half of January, our ponds remained open, supporting numbers of wintering ducks—goldeneyes, buffleheads, mergansers, coots, mallards, and canvasbacks—which ordinarily depart much sooner. But as the ponds began to freeze, the open pools drew tighter and disappeared like drops of water on a hot stove, driving the ducks south or out to open salt water to await a thaw.

And what about the marsh waders—the herons, rails, and egrets that often linger into winter here? What will they do once the salt marshes freeze over, standing on frozen hummocks in the middle of an unfamiliar wasteland, like winter tourists who suddenly find all the motels and restaurants closed?

Even the land birds react to a hard freeze. Our common winter species—chickadees, finches, song sparrows, nuthatches, and jays—as well as northern visitors like kinglets, juncos, pine siskins, waxwings, and evening grosbeaks all seem to work harder, more feverishly, to extract bits of life and warmth from the ground and frozen twigs in the form of scale insects, eggs, seeds, and grubs.

How these small birds cope in the exposed darkness, night after night, I cannot comprehend. Some do not. This morning, I found the incredibly tiny form of a golden-crowned kinglet in the road. A bit of nothing, a pinch of fluff, with its black, pencil-point beak and the hidden flame of scarlet-orange feathers on its crown, a flame that even in death blazed forth when I ruffled it with my fingers. Overhead, a group of his fellows twittered gaily in some bare maple branches, as though to remind me that the design was right, and only the individual inadequate.

The Song of the Scoter

I drove down to the beach for lunch the other afternoon. It was another of those unusually warm, spring-like days that have passed for winter this year. The temperature was in the midfifties, the bay nearly flat calm, and the sun, coming back from exile, sliced the water like ten thousand knives.

The tide was nearly in, forming a wide, azure lake that spread and melted into the distant horizon. Under the bare-naked winter sunlight, flocks of gulls, sea ducks, and black ducks dispersed themselves placidly over the waters. Soft growls, coughs, grunts, and quacks were flowing in over the silken, liquid surface of the bay to the few cars in the parking lot. A single black-bellied plover wheeled and called its mournful whistle at the fringes of the marsh. For a moment, such natural tranquility eclipsed the current domestic and international crises and the recent strandings of dolphins and pilot whales on these shores.

I sat in my car with windows down, just letting the loveliness of the scene wash over me. Bach's Fifth Brandenburg was playing on the radio, turned low to blend with the outside sounds. A young woman, her hair in a red bandana, came up the stairs from the beach. She turned and gave me a broad, open smile, then went to her car.

It was no invitation, even if I had wanted one, but rather, a spontaneous, silent acknowledgment between strangers of the day and the scene we happened to share.

I got out of my car and descended to the beach with my binoculars. A large flock of eiders floated about a hundred yards offshore. There appeared to be some fragmentary courtship-chasing behavior going on among them, but it was all done in a relaxed, languorous manner befitting the day. I could hear the standard eider chatter, the *kuk-kuk-kuks*, like gossip from the females. But every now and then, I heard a soft but distinct whistle, a slow, descending two-note call. I thought at first it might be the plover I had seen back by the car, but this had a soft musicality of tone very different from that shorebird's song. It was a kind of crooning.

Scanning the eiders with my glasses, I spotted a single pair of common, or black, scoters, a smaller sea duck. As I focused on the male scoter, I clearly saw him open his bill and then heard the whistle song a fraction of a second later. I observed this several times, till I was convinced the song came from him.

I was delighted at this novel and unexpected musical performance from a sea duck, but when I mentioned the scoter's song to a couple of experienced local birders I know, neither had ever heard it. After some looking, I finally found a reference to it in Arthur Cleveland Bent's monumental series on the *Life Histories of North American Birds*, published almost a hundred years ago. Bent himself never heard the song, but he quotes one Major Allan Brooks, who wrote: "In fine, calm weather [common scoters] call a great deal and their plaintive cour-loo is the most musical of duck cries."

So there it was: confirmation. But I would have believed my ears and eyes even with no independent corroboration. After all, one should not question the gifts of a day, and my gift, that day, was to hear, for the first and only time in my life, the courting song of the common scoter.

Happy Valentines Day.

Fire and Music

On a cold morning earlier this month, I began to burn the enormous piles of brush that had accumulated from the twenty or so pitch pines I had cut down behind the house last fall. The piles lay like green swells in a bristly sea across the southern slope of our yard. It seemed like a daunting amount of substance to get rid of with a match. But pitch pines live up to their name, and the fresh boughs burned fast and hot.

There is something primally satisfying, even ritualistic, about burning wood—whether brush, logs, or leaves. You build a high pile of combustible, natural matter and ignite it. You wait and watch as the first tendrils of smoke curl and twine together, like a soft, introductory theme. The smoke thickens and ripples, like dark-gray liquid. Then suddenly, the needles catch, glowing a fiery red orange. The flames crescendo, swell, and swirl, sending up great plumes of white-gray smoke and streams of glowing embers into the winter's sky, accompanied by the percussive pops, snaps and crackles of the wood. Then just as quickly, the flames subside, leaving a fretwork of blackened, skeletal branches roasting over a growing pile of glowing coals and ashes below it. You throw on another bough and watch it all over again.

For hours, I hauled and piled bough upon bough onto the flaming pyre. At the end of the day, my eyebrows were singed and my face was burnt by the secondhand sun of combustion. I let the pile burn down as I put away rakes, chainsaw, bucksaws, gasoline, and other paraphernalia of the day's work. Gradually, the shadows lengthened, then disappeared, the sky darkened, and the glowing ash pile was the brightest object in view, a jewel set off by the encroaching night.

I went inside, bathed, and dressed. That evening, I went to the Barnstable High School to hear a concert by the Cape Cod Symphony. It was an all-Rachmaninoff program, played superbly, and I found that the strenuous physical work of the day opened me up to the music in a way I had rarely experienced. Still, one might think that two-and-a-half hours of uninterrupted romanticism would have been excessive. But it wasn't. I couldn't seem to get enough of it. It seemed the perfect music for a winter's night. And I wasn't the only one who felt that way. At the end of the concert, the largely gray-headed, sellout crowd got to its collective feet and cheered like teenagers at a rock concert. It was as if the music had given us back the passions of our youth. And yet, I had the feeling that there was something about *this* particular music that made it so perfect for that evening. But what was it?

And then, there it was, in the program, on

the same page as the notes to the Second Symphony: an uncredited quote, superimposed over a photograph of flames, that read: "Like the embers of a huge log fire, beating back an icy black Russian winter's night, Rachmaninoff's music smolders redly for ages, and occasionally flares, with or without warning, briefly and spectacularly."

The next morning, I went out into the yard and, on the frost-rimed ground, I found a small cone of ashes from yesterday's burning, still smoldering, slowly and unspectacularly.

A Great Good Place

Late one afternoon, on my way home from a medical appointment in Hyannis, I stopped to get a cup of coffee at a donut shop on Route 28. It had no name, just a red neon sign that said Donuts. It had never been a fancy place, but now it looked more stripped down than ever, a commercial victim of the recession, but also one of the last local holdouts against the Dunkin' Donuts juggernaut.

It was a place you might expect to find in the seedier sections of Fall River or Brockton, but not on a main street on Olde Cape Cod. The parking lot had not been swept. The plate-glass windows, though brightly lit inside, were smudged over. The shapes of the figures inside were blurred and obscured. I was drawn to it, as if to a dream.

The glass-enclosed vestibule smelled of old cigarette smoke. Inside, the air was thick and stale, but less than warm. There were about a dozen customers seated at the counter and the orange plastic booths. Most wore tattered quilted jackets and jeans with wool watch caps or baseball caps. The men all had short beards or gray, grizzled chins. At the Formica tables, two pairs of middle-aged men sat playing cribbage, with two or three others looking on from the counter stools. Another man had a *Cape Cod*

Times spread out over his table, the corner held down with coffee in a Styrofoam cup. At a fourth table, a man with Asian features, somewhat better dressed than the others, sat with a younger woman somewhat apart from the rest. If only the windows had been clearer, I thought, this would be a perfect twenty-first-century counterpart to Edward Hopper's famous painting, *Nighthawks*.

I had the odd but distinct feeling that I'd entered someone's house or a private club rather than a public coffee shop. Although hardly anyone spoke, there seemed to be a connection between everyone there. You knew that they all knew one another, knew each other's names, habits, opinions.

The woman behind the counter was probably thirty or thirty-two, but she looked forty-five. She was lean, almost scrawny, with sharp features, stringy, dark hair, and one of her yellowed teeth was prominently missing. She wore maroon pants, a Grateful Dead T-shirt, and a smudged apron.

"What'll it be?" she asked, and I felt tempted to say, "The usual." Instead, I asked for a small coffee, one sugar, and a glazed stick. She brought them, the coffee sweet and syrupy in a Styrofoam cup.

"I could use pennies," she said, as I reached in my pocket for change.

"Most people don't seem to care about

pennies anymore," I said. She didn't rise to the conversational bait, but said simply, "Yeah, but if somebody's change is twenty-four cents, I have to give them pennies."

I could have sat down at the counter for a few minutes and watched the cribbage games with the others, but I knew I'd be intruding, no matter on how little. I found myself thinking of Ray Oldenburg's phrase, "The Great Good Place." That's the title of a book he wrote describing local, public gathering places—cafes, coffee shops, bookstores, bars, hair salons—places where people, unrelated by work or family or even close friendship, come together and interact, forming intermittent and transitory communities that nonetheless fill important social and personal needs. And I saw that, however dingy and perhaps unattractive to outsiders, this, too, was a genuine local gathering place—and it was not mine.

March

An Old Place

A few weeks ago, during a light, late-winter snow, I drove down to one of the bay landings in Brewster, the town I used to live in, to look at the damage that had been done there by recent storms. On the way back to the highway, I passed an old house on the right, next to a former cow pasture. The house was an anomaly even forty years ago when I first knew it, a small, unimposing structure of indeterminate age and jury-rigged additions, seemingly always in a state of general disrepair.

Two women lived in it then, a mother and daughter from an old Brewster family. In good weather, they would sit outside in rocking chairs and among the high, uncut grass, absorbed in some country handwork like sewing or snapping beans. The mother was thin and gray. The daughter was about forty, round bodied, with short, dark hair. She looked something like a Russian doll. She always had a blank look on her face, and some of the locals, in the vernacular of the day, referred to her as "feeble," though others said she had a quick mind.

Even then, the two women seemed to live in another time, in an age of more constricted lives, apart from the rest of the life of the town. They never looked up or even seemed to notice when cars passed them on the way to the beach.

If anyone stopped or even slowed down on their way past, the two women would scatter indoors. I never met them.

Both the women and the cows in the adjacent pasture are long gone, but I was surprised to see that the house is still there. I hadn't been by it in recent years, and I just assumed it had been sold, torn down, or removed, replaced with something more in tune with the times. Perhaps it was the snow that made it stand out to my attention. In any case, it looked unquestionably abandoned, even before I noticed the lack of footprints in the snow, the tendrils of bare euonymus vine tapping at the windows, the several missing panes of glass, the open, flapping side door, and the hole in the back roof.

I stopped the car, left it running, and walked through the low door. It was one of those cheaply built old houses of unexceptional character, a warren of small, dark, low-ceilinged rooms that you felt were never filled with sunlight. There were two old oil heaters, one in the front room and one in the tiny kitchen. Except for a relatively new water heater from Sears, everything in the house seemed to belong to the 1930s or 1940s. There was a sagging, sodden sofa, a thin metal sink, and peeling, water-stained wallpaper. At the back of the house, a set of narrow, steep steps led up to an unfinished second floor containing a gable bedroom with an iron bed frame and a dingy mattress. Everything smelled of mold.

It was the kind of modest, abandoned house I used to come upon occasionally when I first came to the Cape, but which I never expect to find here anymore. Despite its air of impoverished decay, it was somehow refreshing to see a house deconstructing itself, with only the help of the elements, at its own slow pace. I realized I didn't want to see it "saved" and "restored," like all those historic windmills or other old houses you see, made cleaner and brighter and tighter than they ever were in the past. I would rather see it *conserved* as it is: an honestly run-down, dilapidated, falling-in, going-to-ruin old place—a reminder, on our way to the summer beach, of where we came from.

Grace

Lately, I've been reading David McCullough's fine biography of John Adams. Adams was one of the more unpopular of our Founding Fathers. He could be abrasive and tactless. As the character of Ben Franklin says to Adams in the musical *1776*, "You're obnoxious and disliked, you know that's true." But, as McCullough's biography makes abundantly clear, the American Revolution would probably have never taken place without Adams's relentless energy and determination, and his willingness to speak unpopular truths—in this case, the truth that King George would never "reconcile" with or address the colonies' grievances, but would crush them. The colonies, Adams argued, had no choice but to go it alone.

I was struck in particular by one passage that seemed to have an unexpected contemporary ring to it. Writing to his friend James Warren about the Continental Congress in April of 1776, Adams said, "I fear that in every assembly, members will obtain influence by noise, not sense. By meanness, not greatness. By ignorance, not learning. By contracted hearts, not large souls."

As I've listened in recent weeks to the debates, or, more accurately, the shouting matches, over President Obama's health care–reform bill, I can't help but feel there's been an excess of noise, meanness, ignorance, and contracted hearts, and a dearth of sense, greatness, learning, and great souls. I don't take Adams's words so much as prophetic, but rather as enduring observations on human nature and behavior. That is, I'd like to believe that the level of political debate is no worse than it's always been. But to be honest, it's been hard not to feel discouraged by the level of rabid partisanship and the lack of courage among politicians, not to mention the fickle, self-centered, and shortsighted nature of the American electorate itself.

As I sat thinking these dispiriting thoughts, I gazed out the window. I'd been trying to write an essay, but was getting nowhere with it. The skies were clouded over, and large, soft, goose-feather flakes of snow began to fill the air, swirling and drifting like white maple seeds. It wasn't cold enough for the flakes to stick, but it nonetheless seemed miraculous. When I looked at the weather map on my laptop, it showed a soft green cloud of precipitation hovering over the Cape and Islands, like a visitation.

I closed the computer, stood up, and stepped outside on the back porch with only a sweater on. I stood there, letting snowflakes the size of silver dollars alight on my head, hands, and face. They instantly melted, leaving little wet spots of coolness on my skin. I felt a deep and un-expected release of tension, as if I'd received a blessing. I tried to give a name to it: Comfort? Not really. Not exactly balm, either, though it eased my mind. Whatever it was, it was nothing intentional. If there is anything I have learned about nature, it is that it is never intentional—it simply happens.

Nonetheless, I found that standing out in the wet snow brought a profound sense of inner peace. And then I realized what it was: a moment of grace. For what else is nature but trial and grace? And when grace comes—in the form of snowflakes, or three bluebirds at your feeder, or a simple shift in the light—it comes, as grace does, unexpectedly, unasked for, undeserved. Nature's grace is a pure given, transient yet woven into the very fabric of being.

I went inside and got back to work.

Beach Ball

Over the years, I've picked up and carried home from the beach any number of objects—beach stones, shells, lobster buoys, driftwood, odd lengths of rope, unidentifiable bits of flotsam and wreckage, and once, a dead dovekie. Most of these items have lingered on my porch, or in my study, or in my freezer, until I finally discarded them.

But I didn't fully realize the depth and power of the beachcombing urge until one day last month when I arrived at the ocean. I was the only one on the beach. The tide was still low, but coming in. A hundred yards from the parking lot and halfway down the foreslope of the beach sat a large, round, dark object. When I got to it, it proved to be a steel or iron ball. It was about twenty inches in diameter, with a three-inch opening running through the middle of it. It must have weighed at least seventy to eighty pounds. It was obviously hollow, however, and airtight, or it would never have floated up on the beach. I assumed it was some kind of float, perhaps a stabilizer for a light buoy. Well, whatever it was, it had *substance*, and I knew immediately that I had to have it or would at least give every effort, short of a heart attack, to possess it.

I set my shoulder against the ball and began rolling it up the soft, wet beach. Getting it up to the high-tide line wasn't easy, but it was doable. At that point, it occurred to me that I could leave the ball there and go for assistance or even come back the next day. After all, did I really think that someone else would be crazy enough to try to move this useless, heavy object up the beach in my absence? Well, *yes*.

So I put my shoulder to the ball again and rolled it across the wide, flat expanse of upper beach to the base of the slope leading up to the parking lot. Here, there was a fairly steep rise of some ten to twelve feet. I started pushing the ball up the sand path that slanted obliquely down to the beach, but I was only able to move it a few feet at a time before having to stop for breath. At this point, I realized I was inadvertently reenacting the Greek myth of Sisyphus, who was condemned to roll a rock up a steep hill, only to see it roll back down every day. If my object rolled back down the beach, I knew I wouldn't have the strength or the resolve to try it again.

Eventually, however, I managed to roll the ball up the slope and onto the asphalt. I had just enough strength left to hoist it up into the back of my van. I drove the ball to my friend Ralph, who can identify anything. Sure enough, he recognized it as a "bottom roller," part of a fishing trawler's rig that attaches to the bottom of the net to help it roll smoothly across the ocean floor.

I took the ball home and unloaded it at my

house, where it joined what I refer to as my collection of conversational landscape objects. The next day, after it dried out, it gained an unexpectedly lovely patina of golden rust that stretched like water shadows over its surface. It was one of the very few objects I have collected that actually became more beautiful after I brought it home from the sea. But then, I knew it wasn't really from the sea; and it had only been loaned to me for a while.

Postmortem

Earlier this month, there were two strandings of white-sided dolphins in South Wellfleet. Of the twenty-four stranded dolphins, seventeen were eventually rescued and released in an effort co-ordinated by the Cape Cod Stranding Network. I didn't participate in these rescue efforts, though I have been involved in several in the past. In particular, these reminded me of a similar stranding in Wellfleet about a dozen years ago, where, for the first time, I took part in a mercy killing. Three stranded dolphins had been trapped in Duck Creek, in the vicinity of Uncle Tim's Bridge. Two of them were eventually herded out of the creek and into deeper water, but a third had stranded on the back side of Cannon Hill.

When I got there, the tide was out. The three-hundred-pound marine mammal lay on its side, at the extreme high-tide line, thrashing its tail futilely. It did not look happy. It was bleeding from a pectoral fin and had scrapes and small gouges all along its length. The two women in charge, Connie Merigo and Rose Borkowski, were both from the New England Aquarium. Gathered around them were other volunteers, representatives of the media, as well as a number of onlookers, photographing and filming the scene. I was one of them, having been handed a camera by someone from the Center for Coastal Studies, who asked me to record the event for them.

Rose, a marine veterinarian, knelt down beside the dolphin, evaluating its condition. She listened to its heartbeat, checked its eyes, examined its mouth and genitals (it was a female). Eventually she got up and consulted with Connie for a few minutes. Then Connie turned to the crowd and made the following statement: The animal, she said, was "deeply stressed." Without "substantial and extended support," there was little chance it could survive. A decision, therefore, had been made to euthanize it. It was not unlike the kind of decision that medical triage units have to make in war.

Rose asked for "another pair of hands" to help hold the animal still while they injected the solution that would stop its heart. I volunteered, glad not to have to film the procedure. Rose, Connie, and I bent over the dolphin. I held its pectoral fin, and Rose held the tail, warning us to be ready to leap back if it began to thrash.

Connie asked her assistant to prepare the fatal injection. The assistant, a young woman with long, curly hair, drew from one of the medical boxes a pint-sized bottle of blue liquid labeled POISON. She had trouble drawing the liquid from the bottle into the syringe. The cold, she said, had made it quite viscous. She had to put the bottle under her sweater for several minutes before it was warm enough to flow. Finally, she got it into the syringe and handed it to Connie. Connie administered the poison through the dolphin's tail flukes, pushing down hard on the plunger. The dolphin went into a brief flurry, then calmed down. We held on as the blue liquid entered its now-still body. Rose bent her head down again and listened for a heartbeat for several minutes. No one was impatient. "There," she finally said, "I think she's gone."

"You never get used to this," I said to her, more as a statement than a question.

"No," she replied.

When we finally let go of the dolphin and got to our feet, there was a feeling of release in all of us as well. We shook our legs that had gone to sleep, and I realized that, at some point, all of the cameras had stopped.

April

A Calm Day in the Bay

The other day, my friend David offered to take me out in his boat into Cape Cod Bay. Over the past few weeks, there have been sightings of an extraordinary number of endangered right whales feeding in the bay, and we hoped to see some. We couldn't have picked a better day. It was incredibly mild and calm. The ocean had that soft, serene, azure hue that lets you know that winter's back has been definitively broken. We motored out of Wellfleet Harbor and set course due west of Great Island, directly into the heart of the bay. When we got about three miles out, we cut the engines.

The bay had the aspect of a wide Sargasso Sea—glossy calm, shaded a soft silky blue, the air mild and slightly hazy, and everything totally, eerily silent. The impression of the Sargasso Sea was intensified by an extensive, meandering ribbon of floating seaweed at least a mile long off our port bow. I thought it might have been a wind wrack, formed by an imperceptible southwest current of air. The high sun of an early April morning twinkled on the sugar-soft surface of the water. The bay seemed not only silent but strangely empty. Despite the mild weather, we saw no other boats or waterfowl and heard no associated sounds. David said that only a few days ago, when he had last been out here, there had been thousands of scoters, eiders, gannets, and other birds scattered across the bay, squawking up a racket.

But today, the bay had the appearance of a vast pond. We were surrounded by a ring of low, undulating hills—from the dunes of the Provincelands to the Truro cliffs to Great Island to the bulge of the Brewster ridge, the high Sandwich Moraine, and the Manomet Hills to the west—and, like the waters of the bay, they all seemed to wear hints of new spring green.

Eventually, some seals surfaced on the calm waters. They leisurely circled and surveyed us, trailing long wakes through perfumed waters, or else sunned themselves on their backs, light glinting off their shiny, sleek, wet hides. We stood on top of the cabin roof, our legs spread and set, balanced on the slow, gentle rocking of the water. I thought of Ishmael in *Moby Dick*, standing in the crow's nest of the *Pequod* on such a day as this, lulled into philosophical reverie by its motion.

Then, all at once, there was the audible and familiar soft explosion of air signaling a whale blow. We picked up our binoculars and scanned the waters, but could see nothing. In a minute, another blow came, of indeterminate distance and direction. And then we saw it—a long, low, wet glint of light on the surface, like a sword breaking water. Then a third whale spouted further to the north. They must have been two or three miles off, but in the strange silence of the bay, their low, soft breaths had a dimension that made it seem as if the whales were in the same room with us.

A breeze suddenly picked up from the southwest, and the bathtub aspect of the bay disappeared. Small waves began to form on the water, turning it a darker hue. Scattered flocks of waterfowl appeared as if from nowhere in the sky, their cries raining down on us. And it was as if all this had been blown into being by the breath of the whales.

Grouse Crazy Flights

About six o'clock one evening, as we were about to sit down to dinner, there came from the other end of the house a loud *thunk*, as though something had hit a window. I stepped outside to see what the noise was. At first, I saw nothing but a few curled feathers drifting casually along one of the roof eaves. Then, on the ground below the bedroom window, I spotted the limp form of a ruffed grouse.

Even in death, its brown-, black-, and white-flecked plumage was perfect camouflage, blending in with last year's leaves and litter. The grouse had curious, leathery eyelids that seemed to close upwards from the bottom, like a snake's. Pasted on the window, about twelve feet above ground level, a small spot of feathers showed where the bird had struck. It must have been flying directly at the window at considerable speed, for the neck was not only broken, but completely wrenched open, exposing the crop.

Birds crashing into windows are not unusual, and over the years, we have had our share. Putting silhouettes of hawks or owls on picture windows will help prevent these avian accidents, but not completely, for sometimes birds will simply fly into the sides of houses for no apparent reason. The so-called crazy flights of grouse, for instance, are well known, though they usually occur in the fall. At such times, many immature grouse will suddenly take off in a whirring explosion of wings and fly headlong through the woods like feathered runaway locomotives. During such flights, the grouse, usually expert at twisting and dodging through the thickest tangles of briars and branches when flushed, rush blindly forward and frequently collide with posts, tree trunks, and houses.

Some ornithologists think this phenomenon is a dispersal technique, designed to break up large grouse families at the end of summer so that young males can seek out and establish new territories. To my mind, this is a rather inane theory, making as much sense as having young human males establish independent lives by putting on blindfolds and setting off on motorcycles at full throttle.

Another theory suggests that the birds are thrown into a panic by the falling of the leaves, which the young have never seen before. Since many natural enemies of grouse are airborne predators, such as hawks and owls, the immature bird presumably takes the falling, curved, bristle-tipped oak leaves for a thousand descending claws, and it understandably panics. If there's anything to this idea, it must be a nightmare experience for the young grouse, a vision of universal predation, as though, walking across your lawn, all of the blades of grass turned suddenly into vipers.

But these "crazy flights," whatever their origins, do not normally occur in spring. A more likely explanation for this casualty was that the grouse, seeing the sky and limbs of nearby trees reflected in the window glass, had taken it for an extension of the woods from which it had just emerged and had been killed instantly.

I took up the bird and brought it into the house, where we admired its beauty and commiserated over its untimely death. I was sorry to have been even indirectly responsible for it, for grouse populations on the Cape have been declining drastically in recent decades due to the breakup of undisturbed woodland for development. We cannot spare any of the remaining ones, especially during the breeding season.

It was a sad and regrettable fate for such a proud, handsome bird. I carried it out into the woods and laid it gently on top of a stone wall as a kind of spring offering to whatever local foxes or coyotes might be emerging for a night's hunt. Then I returned to the house and sat down to dinner.

Sea Dawn

For some time, I've been waiting for an excuse to tell you about a very unusual object in our driveway. Now that I finally have a reason, I wish I didn't. The object in question is a boat. Specifically, it's the thirty-five-foot wooden hull of a racing schooner built in 1929 and named *Sea Dawn*. *Sea Dawn* had several owners and eventually made her way to Wellfleet. In the late 1980s, it was acquired by Kim and Phillipe Villard, the people who built our house. They were building a sailboat of their own in the driveway and acquired *Sea Dawn* for parts. After they'd stripped her, they managed to turn the hull over and set it up on wood pilings to serve as a rather unique carport.

In the years since we have lived here, the large upside-down hull of *Sea Dawn* has provided a durably interesting anecdote to tell to visitors, a landmark for UPS deliverers, and a magnet for our neighbor's young children, Clemmie and Lyle, who think it would make a great clubhouse. But two weeks ago, the boat became part of a tragic local story that has left a hole in this community. On April 1, Jan Potter, a longtime resident, master builder, and well-known figure in Wellfleet, took his own life at Newcomb Hollow Beach. The story has been reported in the media, and it's not my intention to dwell on it here. I simply want to speak of my connection to Jan, which was not unusual or notable except in one regard.

I knew Jan for many years, though we were not close friends. On the other hand, he was something more than an acquaintance. I frequently saw him at the local coffee shop, where he always had a friendly and slightly ironic greeting. We spent several late evenings in the local bar watching Red Sox games together. Ours was, at most, a casual friendship, the kind that local gathering places foster without imposing any of the responsibilities or obligations of close friends. But it was real nonetheless, one of those informal but reliable relationships that make you feel you belong to a genuine community. Last summer, when Jan's oldest son, Caleb, suffered life-threatening injuries in a skateboarding accident, Kathy and I, along with the rest of the town, rallied around Jan and his family as best we could, because that is what a community does.

The boat, however, gives me a tangible connection to Jan that I value even more now. For you see, one summer years ago, Jan and his young family lived on *Sea Dawn* in Wellfleet Harbor, and it was from Jan that Kim and Phillipe acquired her. Last fall, I put a long-contemplated plan into effect and closed in the space beneath the hull to make a workshop out of it. It was something I thought Jan would approve of. In fact, when

I rather proudly told him about it, he did seem pleased. I said he should stop by and see it some time. He said he would, and seemed to mean it. He never did.

But there was another, even more remarkable connection. Two days after Jan's death, our neighbor, Galen Malicoat, the mother of little Clemmie and Lyle, who have so frequently visited that boat, gave birth to a new son, Ryland James. It was a home birth, with the aid of her husband, Beau, and two midwives. It was an easy delivery, and mother and son are doing very well.

As a confirmed rationalist, I don't believe in cosmic alignment. But the juxtaposition of these two events, one so dark, the other full of light, seems to stretch the bounds of coincidence. As I contemplate the nexus of death and birth that somehow gathered around *Sea Dawn*, there comes unbidden into my mind the words of Laura Nyro's great anthem from the late 1960s: "And when I die, and when I'm gone / There'll be one child born and a world to carry on, to carry on."

Woodcock Flight

Each year around this time, I go to a small, grassy clearing near our house to witness one of the most remarkable yet least observed of the Cape and Island's spring spectacles: the courtship flight of the American woodcock. Almost everything about the woodcock is a curious mixture, a contradiction in terms. To start with, ornithologists describe the woodcock as "an upland shorebird." It has a peculiar anatomy that is the consequence of forsaking its ancestral habitats of mud flats and salt marshes for inland forests. It's about the size of a man's fist, with short legs and neck. It has large, black, shoe-button eyes set far back in the head. Its bill is almost three inches long and full of sensitive nerve endings that aid the bird in finding its staple food, earthworms. The woodcock uses its bill to probe the wet soil, detecting the movement of worms.

And yet the strangest things about this squat, drab, mud-poking curiosity of adaptation is its courtship flight, one of the most beautiful aerial displays in the avian world. But unless you know something about its habits, you're likely never to experience it. The woodcock is notoriously elusive, and the spectacle is a muted one. It's a twilight flight, a crepuscular ballet that takes place on the teasing edge of visibility about a half hour after sunset or an hour before dawn, anytime between early April and late May.

The courting or singing ground of the woodcock is usually some open field, or even a suburban lawn, surrounded by young trees and some low, woody cover, often near a wet or boggy area used for feeding. The small field I go to possesses all these elements and is perfect woodcock courting territory. I approach the area cautiously and wait just across the road from the field. I sit quietly, facing the fading light, and listen closely in the gathering dusk. I wait. And wait. Then, as the evening chirps and twitters of other songbirds gradually subside into a roosting silence, I hear it: a new note, not a bird sound at all, but a strange, buzzing, insect-like "*peent........peent.*"

The male woodcock is warming up. These calls previous to flight always remind me of the wide-spaced spurts of a prop-airplane motor being turned over. They continue for ten minutes or so, at first coming at long intervals, but gradually increasing in frequency and urgency, until suddenly, from the dark, low ground, the bird erupts on whirring wings and becomes a rapidly moving silhouette, a dark, whistling form like a giant bumblebee, against the last light of sunset.

He takes off at a low angle, moving out swiftly beyond the ring of trees, wings whistling through the air, circumscribing the horizon in low, sweeping arcs, gradually rising higher and higher in contracting spirals until, at the apex, he disappears near a star.

Then the motor begins to miss, and an intermittent choke-like chirping is heard—the "true song" of the woodcock. The bird folds his wings, and the dark, squat mass plummets like a spirit spent and broken down to the ground below, landing near the spot where he took off. Almost immediately, the male woodcock begins *peent*ing again, and the whole ritual is repeated over and over until full darkness sets in.

There's something very poetic about these nocturnal flights, a fragile extravagance and a moth-like grandeur. Yet there's also something mechanical, almost humorous. In sum, the woodcock courtship flight strikes me as a strange avian mixture of Shelley and the Wright brothers.

A Gratuity

Every week, it seems, there is another story about the decline of newspapers or the closing of another major daily. The stories document the economic reasons for this, while editorials bemoan the loss of substantial investigative journalism. Essayists and op-ed writers eulogize the tactile qualities and the rituals of reading an ink-and-paper news sheet.

I am one of those who find it as difficult to start the day without a printed newspaper in my hand as without the cup of hot coffee or tea in the other, yet till now, I've not felt I had anything new to offer to the discussion. But the other day, I was reminded of another benefit of print newspapers that I had not thought of before: my "delivery person." Newspapers must be delivered, and they must be delivered by a real individual. If you're like me, chances are you've never met your newspaper "delivery person," the term that has now replaced the iconic "paper boy" of previous eras (as single mothers and retirees in cars have largely replaced the boys on bicycles as the deliverers). Newspapers are delivered—or are supposed to be—before most of us are up in the morning. So we have little or no personal contact with our newspaper deliverer and probably never think of her or him except when there is a missed or late delivery, or when we have to pick a soaked, unwrapped paper out of a mud puddle.

Over the decades, we've had many "delivery persons" of varying quality and reliability, but for the past couple of years, we have had a gem. Like the previous ones, I've never met her, but I know her name: Susanna. Susanna has been more reliable and timely than any of her predecessors. Her Christmas cards contain a personal note that previous ones have lacked. Her papers are always carefully wrapped, or double-wrapped if the weather warrants it, and so rarely is the paper delivered late that, when it occurs, I tend to assume the delay was caused by something beyond her control.

The other day, we got with the newspaper one of those forms that are included periodically. The form asks if there is "anything we can do to improve upon our service?" and concludes, "Many subscribers have also asked how they can reward their delivery person for quality service. If you feel a gratuity is appropriate, you may use the enclosed envelope for that purpose as well."

I don't know why exactly, but this time the form made me think, concretely, about the job Susanna does. Most of the year, every morning, seven days a week, she gets up before dark, goes to the depot where her papers are delivered, wraps each one in a plastic bag, drives around several towns in all kinds of weather for several hours before beginning her day job or house chores. I don't know how much she makes (probably not much), or whether the job includes any benefits (highly doubtful), but having been a part-time postal deliverer myself, I know how wearing on both bodies and vehicles such a job can be.

Even more, her service provides me with a real connection with a real human being, even if I've never met her. I *depend* on her for something small but important to my day, and, with few exceptions, she has not disappointed me. Every morning, I find that small (alas, increasingly small) plastic-wrapped package at the end of our driveway, and when I do, it seems like a little personal gift from Susanna.

I know that in all likelihood we are both playing a losing game, and that one day, not too far off, our connection will probably cease. When it does, I hope it will be because Susanna has found a better job. But in the meantime, it is a connection that provides me with more than the physical newspaper I open over tea and bagels, and so I write out a check in Susanna's name, put a stamp on the envelope provided, and place it in that other artifact of a vanishing culture: the mailbox.

May

Snapper

On the way home from town last week I saw a large, dark object in the middle of the road. I stopped the car and got out to look at it. It was a snapping turtle, the first of the season, and a whopper. Nearly two-feet long, it had a dark-brown, crusty shell, a large, scaly head with a hooked, hawk-like beak, claws for feet, and a long, dragging, serrated tail. Its appearance was impressively ferocious, except for its eyes. The eyes—those deep, shiny, dewy-fresh eyes of reptiles, so startling in their ancient, scaly bodies—looked perplexed, not frightened exactly, but lost in an impersonal way, as if trying to get their bearings.

There, where the turtle straddled the road, a freshwater swamp lay on either side. In its twenty-five-million-year-old trek from one swamp to another, it had suddenly found itself on a modern highway, an asphalt strip that bisected its world with no points of reference. It stood bewildered, its roots momentarily cut. It was queer to think that such a small and exploited land as ours can still harbor such apparitions as this strange and ancient bit of reptilian life.

I went over and picked it up carefully by the back edge of the shell. I thought briefly of taking it to the Audubon sanctuary, and even more briefly of turtle soup. But as it turned its snake-like head and stared back at me with that impersonal, insulated gaze, I realized what I really wanted was to stay there and talk to it, to hold what converse we could manage across our vertebrate class lines—to talk turtle, for once. If nothing else, I felt that I might gradually absorb from it a patient readiness for thought, saying nothing, but suddenly striking out in purposive action.

But as I held it there, like a divining rod above the heated highway, I realized how clogged our lines of communication were with myth, prejudice, and irrational fears. The snapping turtle, an American native, bears one of the most complex relationships to humans of any reptile. Iroquois Indians used the dried shells as rattles and drums in ceremonial dances. In New England, it used to be common for families to keep a snapper in a hog-swill barrel until it was fat enough to transfer to the soup pot.

Yet its appearance and formidable striking capabilities have given the snapper an unfortunate and ill-deserved reputation. Turtle literature almost invariably describes it as "savage," "voracious," "mean," "sullen"—in a word, a bad character. For generations, children were taught that these "vicious" snappers drag cute, helpless ducklings down to a watery death and chomp off the toes and fingers of unwary swimmers. In many areas, such ingrained ignorance led to attempts to exterminate this reptile.

Fortunately, modern herpetologists have come to the defense of this much-maligned beast. This "ravenous" carnivore actually consumes much more vegetable matter and carrion than animal life, and its "ferocious" behavior exists largely on land—that is, when provoked while out of its normal habitat. In the water, the snapper tends to avoid humans. You are much more likely to be attacked by a swan than a snapping turtle.

But the snapper's eyes seemed to say to me that whatever moral I wanted from it, I would have to draw myself. So I set the turtle down on the other side of the highway and watched it zigzag off, dragging its Stegosaurian tail through the grass down into the shallow swamp, where it settled slowly from sight like a wide stone.

Valley of the Foxes

I first found the Valley of the Foxes over a dozen years ago. Like Shangri-La, I stumbled upon it while following three deer that bounded down the side of a long, steep drop-off into a deep, enclosed valley perhaps five-hundred-feet long. The valley slopes were covered with mature pine woods and the floor was open and glade-like. At one end was a small water hole, with long grass growing in its center and dozens of deer and other animal prints around its edge. Exploring this unexpected find, I found a freshly dug fox den—a large, splayed fan of fine, new, yellow sand. I knelt down to the entrance of the dark hole and caught a whiff of strong, musky, wet-dog fox odor. After that, I visited the valley sporadically, occasionally finding more fresh fox dens but never actually catching a glimpse of one of these elusive animals.

Then, one day in early May, I brought my friend Sherry there with me. Sherry is a professional masseuse, and for several years, we had had a nice barter arrangement: I took her on nature walks in exchange for massages. The length and quality of the massage varied loosely in direct proportion to that of the walk. We each thought we had the better of the deal.

We entered the valley by way of the water

hole and made our way across some fallen trunks, walking along them like balance beams. Then I spied a bare patch about halfway up the south slope. Training my binoculars on it, I saw two fox pups, playing at the entrance to the den. They were big, fluffy, healthy-looking kits, their legs black to the knees, a white patch on each tail. They scrambled and rolled over one another, and were apparently completely unaware of us.

We watched them gamboling for fifteen minutes or so, handing the glasses back and forth and making whispered commentaries to one another. Sometimes, the pups would stop playing and root about in the loose sand in front of the den or would venture a few yards from the opening, but no farther.

At last, we continued on, satisfied that we had seen what we had come to see. But after another hundred feet or so, Sherry noticed another movement on the slope ahead of us. There, on approximately the same level as the first den and some two hundred feet east of it, was a second den, this time with three fox pups playing and rambling in front of it, perfect copies of the first pair in size and appearance. They also seemed completely unaware of us, though we were now careful in our movements.

I had never heard of two active fox dens so close together, and Sherry kidded me about having placed trained or robot animals there in order to guarantee myself an extraordinary massage. But my guess was that the pups all belonged to the same litter and that the mother was in the process of relocating them to a new den—which is something that commonly happens if the adult senses a threat.

Finally we stopped watching, sated at last with enough of a good thing, and began making our way out of the valley. As we walked back to the car, we debated whether we should tell others about the experience or leave the foxes undisturbed. Sherry said she probably would bring her husband and three children back the next day, with a video camera. I wasn't so sure. And anyway, I was too busy contemplating my next massage.

Lost Roads

When I first came to live on Cape Cod nearly four decades ago, one of the main roads running from my town to the adjoining one was still a dirt cart track several miles long. It ran through unbroken and undeveloped woods, except for a short portion of it that had been widened and paved where it crossed the Mid-Cape Highway. The road was said to be over two hundred years old. Along stretches of it, the traffic of centuries had worn down the sandy soil five or six feet below the level of the bordering forest, as a river wears down its bed.

This cartway had long served as the major thoroughfare between two villages, but modern automobiles found it faster and more comfortable to take the roundabout route on paved highways. Still, I occasionally enjoyed driving over it, just for the ride. It was like taking a short trip back in time, or at least affirming an old direction. In late spring, the branches of the young oaks arched overhead, dappling the road with sun and shadow. Long fern fronds reached out, brushing the sides of my car like carwash scrubbers as I passed. I traveled slowly, not only because of the constrictions of the road, but because it seemed appropriate and more than possible that around the next turn I might meet one of the old, blue-painted Cape wagons, with their wide-rimmed wheels, churning its slow way through the sandy ruts.

Even then, of course, a road like this was a symbol of something passing, already as insubstantial as the ghosts that lingered along its borders. Within a few years, like so many of our old dirt roads, it had been obliterated, replaced by a broad, paved highway as straight as a drag strip, which is what it is now frequently used as by local teenagers. Streetlights and power lines now line the road, replacing the trees and ferns, and subdivisions and golf courses sprawl along its length.

Good people, I'm sure, still live along this road, but I don't see how they can feel any kinship with it anymore. It's no longer a thoroughfare, a human figure traced through a particular setting, but rather an abstract, asphalted alley, good not for traveling on, but only for getting from one place to another. Such roads serve as sensitive barometers of our relationship to the land as a whole. It's the same for the passing of an old road as for a culture. As more and more old roads are "improved," they increasingly reflect the anonymity of those who pass over them. An old road has character in that it is recognizable. It reflects its setting and possesses that elusive quality we call "a sense of place." A Cape Cod road does not look the same as a Vermont Mountain road, or a Maine Coast road, or a Connecticut Valley road.

For that matter, a Wellfleet road does not look the same as a Nantucket road or a Chilmark road.

In earlier times, travelers arriving were greeted with questions about their trip. They talked about what they saw and did on their journeys, as each was likely to be different. Now, we generally ask only "Did you have any trouble?" and talk only about how little or how much time it took us to drive or fly from one point to another—as though the virtue of any trip lay mainly in how little we had the opportunity to see.

Perhaps, as the proponents of progress insist, our salvation does lie in our mobility and traveling light, in which case these old dirt cartways and narrow, winding roads are merely inconvenient impediments. But before we let too many of them disappear, this much should be said for old roads and their travelers: For as long as people have made journeys, pleasure in old age has been in remembering obstacles overcome rather than conveniences enjoyed. It may take us a generation or two of uneasy boredom shuttling along interstate highways and wide, straightened roads to admit it, but I suspect that, in the end, we still prefer to make our way rather than merely travel it.

Diner

On holiday weekends, I usually manage to find an excuse to head off-Cape. This year, my brother-in-law got us tickets to a Red Sox game, but last year, my desire to escape the hordes of Memorial Day weekend visitors led to an expected discovery.

That Friday, a little before 2 p.m., I decided to explore some of the mainland's back roads. I got off I-195 at the Route 28 exit and headed toward Middleboro. Within a mile or so, on my right, I came upon Sisson's Diner, "Est. 1926." There was a pickup and a green-and-white Safari Classic Harley motorcycle parked outside. I've been a diner aficionado all my life, so of course I stopped and went inside.

I could see as soon as I entered that this was the real thing, not a "reproduction," not even just an authentic old diner, but an actual altered trolley car, the source of the original roadside diners. The main section of the diner was only eight feet wide. A long counter with revolving stools ran down the middle, with a small, single table at each curved end. The floor was a classic pattern of black-and-white linoleum. The ceiling, made of exposed matchboard paneling, had a long, narrow row of clerestory windows on each side.

As I came in, the man with the pickup got up

from one of the tables and left. The diner owner was a man of about sixty who introduced himself as Nick the Greek. He wore a stained apron and spoke with a thick accent. He told me he had worked at the Mattapoisett Diner as a cook for twenty-one years and had bought this place, Sisson's Diner, three years ago. "Used to be good," he said. "Not so much now. The locals, they don't come here anymore. This isn't what they want."

Maybe not, but it was definitely what I wanted. The walls were covered with handwritten menu items, the usual diner fare: all-day breakfasts (a must), sandwiches and wraps, pasta dishes. A large piece of cardboard stuck on the wall behind the counter announced the day's special: "Spaghetti—Served w/ sauce—$4.95."

I ordered a bacon cheeseburger with onions and fries. When Nick brought my burger, he had forgotten the onions, but the fries were some of the best I've ever had—hand-cut, thick, but not too thick. Crunchy on the outside and soft on the inside, redolent and succulent with animal fat. When I complimented him on the fries, he said, "Yeah, I hear that a lot."

Except for the flat-screen computer register, everything in the place bespoke a time warp. Nick himself might have been a character out of a Bernard Malamud story from sixty years ago. "This diner was made by the Buzzards Bay Trolley Co.," he told me, "and it used to run right by here, from Buzzards Bay to Middleboro. I've got a coin, you know, a token I found behind one of the walls. It says 'Buzzards Bay Trolley Co.' on it. But then the buses came along and ruined it."

He showed me more—how on the wood paneling above where the driver's seat would have been was painted a faded, cracked number, "229." "See, that was this car's number." Above it was some ancient, braided-fabric wiring with ceramic insulators, around which he had installed new wiring.

He went back into the kitchen, but after a few minutes, with no one else in the place, he came back out front and, without prompting, began to tell me his life story.

As a young man, he had sailed with the merchant marine, going all over the world: China, Japan, Africa—always picking up information on local food. He loved to talk about food. We discussed baccalieu, or cod, and the many different recipes for it around the world, from Newfoundland to Sicily. "In the north places," he said, "they use pork fat to give it some flavor, but also it's cold there, and people need something to burn in them. In the south, we've got things growing all year long—you plant something and it's there. You get so many flavors you just go crazy."

It had been his dream to have a place of his own, and when he bought this place, he didn't realize that what he had was a genuine trolley car. He had taken down a false ceiling and exposed the original matchboards himself. "There was a headlight on the front of the car," he said, "and when I took it off, the metal case said 1896, so this place is well over one hundred years old."

When I had finished my sandwich, he took me into the added-on back section that contained a half-dozen tables and pointed to a calendar on the wall that depicted a dozen or more "Diners of Eastern Massachusetts," including several from the Worcester area, Lynn, Wareham, Mattapoisett, and of course, Sisson's in South Middleboro. His was the only one that had been a real trolley car, and he said it was the second-oldest diner in the state.

"But people don't appreciate old things anymore," he said. "The locals used to come in here, but now it's mostly road traffic, like you, and not much of that. And people don't act decent no more. One woman thought she had been insulted by the waitress, so I come up to her to, you know, see what the problem was and she says, 'F--- you!' to my face. Now what's that? Can't we talk about things no more?"

In one of the best backhanded compliments I've ever heard, he told me that one of his regulars once said to him, "I hope that when you die, you go to hell so that you can continue cooking food for me."

I couldn't help but think that most places

like this, and most people like Nick the Greek, are either gone or in museums. From the state of the place, and the lack of customers, even on a holiday weekend, the diner didn't seem like a long-term proposition. Nick himself seemed to acknowledge this, saying, "Maybe if I can get enough money together, I'll go look for a place in Connecticut."

I noticed a number of photos on the wall, showing bikers in full leather gear in front of the diner. Nick told me that was his Harley parked outside. "Oh yeah," he said, "we hold a Vintage Motorcycle Rally here at the diner on the last Sunday in May every year. You ought to come back to see it." I said I'd like to. When I left, another pickup was pulling in behind me.

June

Like most children in the Eastern United States, I grew up thinking that trees grew everywhere. I thought this despite my school geography lessons and all the Westerns and biblical desert movies I watched as a kid, because, after all, everywhere that *I* went, I saw trees.

I grew up in northeastern New Jersey, in the urban shadow of Newark—nobody's idea of a sylvan paradise. And yet, even along the cracked sidewalks of my childhood, trees were always at hand, not just as shady presences, but literally, and somewhat illicitly, *at hand*. Each spring, I remember, my friends and I sought out the crooked-branched, black-plated trees that seemed to grow in almost every backyard, playground, or park. Climbing up their rough trunks, we stripped the fruiting branches of their small, hard, green berries, which made perfect ammunition for the peashooters that appeared each spring in our corner store. It was decades before I learned that these "pea trees," as we called them, were actually Black Cherries.

No less useful were the stunted, thorny trees we found in vacant lots—trees, it seemed, that would grow anywhere. Their sprouts, shooting up among junk and trash, made superb bows for our Cowboy and Indian games. And their weird fruit—large, warty, globular green spheres the size of softballs—were filled with acrid-smelling milky pulp. We called them stink bombs, and they were perfect for summer snowball fights. We might have taken more pride in our makeshift archery if we'd known that this tree was highly valued for making bows by the Osage Indians of Arkansas and Missouri, a tribe from which the tree got its more familiar common name: Osage Orange.

And then there was the fall ritual of helping our fathers rake the nameless, numberless leaves that fell from the nondescript trees in our front yards and along the sidewalks. We heaped them into great piles along the gutters in the street and then—miraculously—set them ablaze in the crisp, early darkness of October evenings. The piles of burning leaves sent plumes of pungent, acrid smoke into the air, smells that seared themselves into the deep crevices of my memory. It's a memory that even now seems not just environmentally innocent, but curiously and powerfully primitive.

I mention these early childhood experiences with trees because they contain not just an irony, but a deep paradox. Every one of these boyhood activities is now either illegal or environmentally incorrect. Peashooters have been outlawed for decades. I haven't seen a stink-bomb fight since—well, since I was a boy. And autumn leaves, of course, are now sanitarily packed in plastic bags and hauled off to be buried in some landfill, there to slowly burn by oxidation, invisible and unwitnessed.

As a child of cities, I was in my twenties before I could tell the difference between a maple and an oak, or saw any need to. Over the years, I've come to recognize and be able to identify most local tree species. Moreover, I've learned a great deal about their biology, their chemistry, their ecology, and their environmental importance as "carbon sinks," among other things. Yes, I know a lot more about trees now than I used to, but I also wonder if, in gaining that knowledge, I've also lost something, something of the intimate contact, predatory appreciation, and carnal knowledge I had of them as a child—before, like Adam, I gave them names.

Tern, Eel, Wind, Sun

After paddling hard in Nauset Harbor for an hour or so, I ended up on the inside of the barrier beach, about one hundred yards south of the inlet. It was a little after noon. I beached the canoe, unpacked my binoculars, and spent the next hour and a half watching the least tern colony from outside the perimeter of the nesting area posted with signs.

It is a large colony here, a half mile long by about six hundred feet wide, with nests scattered widely over this wagging tongue of sand. The nests are mere scrapes in the sand and difficult to spot. In fact, the protection of a least tern's nest lies in its very exposure, its lack of definition, its pure anonymity. It does not conceal itself, like, say, the yellowthroat's small, conical nest woven into the center of a viburnum bush. Rather, it shares the lack of concealment, the constant exposure that characterizes this environment. Like the beach, the nests stare back blankly at the observer, and so they are not seen.

In the few nests I spotted, there were only eggs, no chicks, always two to a nest. They varied greatly in color from light to dark brown, sea green, fawn, and soiled ivory. I did not stay long at any one point, to avoid keeping the terns off their nests, since exposure can also be lethal to the eggs or young chicks. Though it was relatively cool and breezy, the sand burned my feet, and I had to bury them several inches below the surface in order to stand in one place for more than a few seconds. I placed my palm down into a nearby beach-buggy track, where young chicks often seek refuge if disturbed, and found that it was much hotter in the track than on the surrounding sand.

Least terns flew up at my approach and made gentle assaults as I passed, uttering high *kivy* calls. I saw one, at the center of the colony, with a large sand eel, five or six inches long, held crosswise in its beak. The sand eel was nearly as long as the bird. It didn't seem to know quite what to do with it. It shook it, like a hawk shaking a snake, put it down on the sand, picked it up again, and finally flew off with it.

Other terns dove into the channel west of the inlet, hovering seven or eight feet in the air on whirring wings and fanned-out tails. They dropped like arrows beneath the fast-sliding currents, emerging a few seconds later like born-again angels. I have watched these graceful birds many times diving into creeks and offshore waters, coming up with coiling silver ropes in their mouths that flash in the sun. Their vision, in this respect, is much more refined than mine, since they not only have to pick these fish out beneath a sparkling, broken water surface, but must also correct for water refraction in their dives.

It's not surprising that these two organisms— tern and sand eel—locked in an elemental relationship for geological ages, have each become such sculpted, refined representatives of their respective mediums. Over the millennia, the sand eel's form has become less and less discernible in the water, the tern's eye keener, the eel more supple and elusive, the tern more adept and skillful in pursuit, and so on, until—what? Until the fish move like wind and sun and the tern can catch light itself.

Mimosa

I'm sitting on our second-story deck this morning, writing, as the delicate, feather-like leaflets of the mimosa tree reach out to me. In the light breeze, they seem almost animate, as if I can see them growing toward me before my eyes. It wouldn't surprise me, for rarely, if ever, have I ever known anything to respond so quickly, so fully, so richly, and so unexpectedly to the minimal encouragement I have given this tree.

For the first six years we lived here, the mimosa was barely more than a tall bush, its growth stunted under the thick shade of several tall pitch pines. My friend Laura suggested that I "liberate" it by opening it up to the sun, so three summers ago, I cut down the smallest pine that was directly overshadowing it. By the following spring, the mimosa began to spread, and by the solstice, it had welled up almost to the level of the deck, extending its spindly branches at least two feet during the season. By the end of that summer, it had filled up most of the available new space.

Encouraged by this unexpected response, I cut down several more pines, creating a small natural amphitheater in which the mimosa's amazing growth continued the following summer. During May and June, the tree almost doubled in size again. Its upper branches climbed to twelve feet in height, topping the deck rail. The horizontal growth was even more impressive, spreading more than fifteen feet from the two-inch-wide trunk. Now, only two years after I first liberated it to the light, the mimosa tree has established itself as a new and significant presence in my daily experience.

This summer, the mimosa seems less a tree and more a multilevel fountain, the expression of a green force that will rise and fill up whatever space is allowed to it. It possesses an exotic, emerald hue that stands out against the darker, mature foliage behind it. All summer long, it retains the green-gold color of spring, giving it a sense of perpetual freshness and youth, an effect enhanced by the fine delicacy of its leaves and the spare elegance of its spreading limbs.

When the sun pours down on the leaves after ten o'clock, the tree seems to actually *glow*, to possess an inner luminescence, or iridescence, like the green plumage of tropical parrots. This effect of having its own inner light is enhanced by the sunlight passing through its translucent and finely slitted leaves, bathing the lower branches and trunk in a green, underwater light. When I look down from the deck above it, through its complex tracery of leaves and shadows of leaves, it is as if I were looking down into an ever-shifting, emerald, tropical sea.

The tree is hardly ever still, for its fine, sensitive,

compound leaflets respond to the least whisper of a breeze. In fact, the movement of the tree possesses that same fascinating movement of surf pouring over half-sunken rocks on the ocean coast, a symphony of motion, endlessly complex, unpredictably repetitive, seemingly chaotic yet unified by the interplay of its form and the forces acting upon it.

As I write these words, the tips of the mimosa leaves reach over the deck rail and dip lightly and repeatedly in faint breaths of wind. They seem like the gloved fingers of an elegant and dignified lady tut-tutting me in tolerant and affectionate reprimand of my overfondness, my overwilling-ness to make too much of her qualities. But it is no use; I am smitten.

Dune Swale

At the very tip of Cape Cod lies the dune country of the Provincelands, an area of about three square miles. It is a visually spectacular place, stunning in its Sahara-like sweep of moving sands. Equally impressive, though, is the remarkably varied patchwork of separate regions and distinct spaces it contains, each with its own character and charms. Because of this variety of habitats, the whole area seems much larger than its narrow boundaries would at first suggest. This is true of the mounded and chaotic hillocks and depressions of the Snake Hills in the western part of the Provincelands and of the broad, majestic bowls of the Parabolic Dunes to the east.

But perhaps the greatest diversity of environments occurs in the "core" or middle area of the dunes that lies between Race Point and Pilgrim Lake. Here, the characteristic ridge-and-valley topography of the central dunes predominates, creating alternating landscapes of high, sandy dune ridges and broad, forested valleys or swales. The valleys are generally less explored than the dune ridges, but it is here, on the floor of one of these wooded swales, that one feels most removed and separate from the man-made world. And within each of these dune swales are a number of miniworlds or microhabitats: cranberry bogs, freshwater pools, wide, sandy bowls, and the miniature forests of pitch pine and scrub oak.

The largest of these forested valleys is known as the Great Swale. It is over a mile in length and lies right in the middle of the Provincelands. At one point, the sand jeep trail descends steeply into this sunken oak-and-pine ravine. Although it is only about one hundred fifty feet wide, walking into it is like entering a rich, inland woods where deer, rabbits, snakes, fox, coyotes, owls, towhees, catbirds, pine warblers, and other woodland denizens roam. This time of year, the needle-laden ground is sprinkled with hundreds of tiny, single-blossomed star flowers and the occasional pink lady's slipper.

Once, walking my dog Ollie through the very bottom of this forested enclosure, I found a large box turtle in the grass, not an animal one usually associates with the dunes. Its fiery red eyes glowed and, unlike most box turtles I have encountered, it did not seem intimidated by our approach. In fact, it was Ollie who seemed nonplussed. He barked furiously at the turtle, while crouching a safe distance away. He adopted what I call his ambivalent fight-and-flight posture. Planting his rear feet firmly in the ground behind him, he advanced aggressively with his forelegs. The result was that he gradually stretched himself out, like some cartoon dog, until he fell flat on his stomach.

Here, in this little island of forest surrounded by dunes, the turtle's world seems very circumscribed. But it is also remarkably complete and sufficient. There's plenty of fresh water to drink in the little bog pools, numerous insects, grubs, and mushrooms to eat. For this most terrestrial of turtles, the hissing of the blowing sand grains on the pine needles may seem only a dry rumor of rain as it moves and shifts its shell slowly through the dark, quiet woods and goes silently about the work of the world.

Thunderstorm

I spent my adolescent years in the Midwest, the land of violent thunderstorms, and I miss the air-shattering, bone-jarring cloudbursts that frequently punctuated our muggy summer days. Summer thunderstorms are relatively rare on the Cape and Islands compared with the mainland. The reason is the moderating influence of the ocean. The formation of thunderheads—those dark, towering, anvil-shaped columns of cloud known as cumulonimbus—are formed by the rapid upward convection of great masses of warm, moist air from the ground. The small amount of land mass on the Cape and Islands and the cool ocean air limit such buildups, and sea breezes usually disperse the thunderheads when they do form.

When a good storm does come our way, I try to savor it to the full, like lamb chops on my birthday, gnawing the bones clean and sucking out all the marrow, for who knows when it may come again? So, when the first of the season's thunderstorms arrived in early June, I decided to give it my full and undivided intention.

Around 6 p.m., I became aware of flashes, intermittent and faint, outside the open window. Gradually, the bursts of light grew nearer and brighter until it looked as if incendiary bombs were being dropped out in the bay. Then low grumbles of sound began to trail reluctantly after the flashes. In the yard, the trees began to stir in a light wind.

I shut off the light and sat in the dark, watching the approach of the storm. It was a formal approach, drawing closer in measured, steady, stately stages, like a regal procession. The flashes of light pealed like bugles, growing ever nearer and more brilliant. Reedy gusts of cool air began rushing through the branches, through the open window, and against my face in palpable waves. The muffled flashes continued, and at length, one of them broke out into a textured crackle.

The storm instantly went from rumbles of undefined fluctuations to a fully realized event. Lightning flashes broke out in blinding, sharp strobes, illuminating the yard in blanched shudders of light before collapsing back into blackness. Hard on the lightning's heels came the full-blown thunder: long, geared slides of sound, staggered descents, and rough, ragged blossoms of noise, all overlapping in extended volleys that seemed endless, like the surf.

Never before had I appreciated how fully thunder gives shape to lightning, how its tearing, unfolding architecture brings into relief the charged stairs of the lightning's descents. When the negatively charged ions in a thundercloud break down into the electrical spark we call a lightning bolt, the air column surrounding it is heated and expands rapidly. It is this expansion of air that creates the shock waves we hear as thunder. Thunder, in other words, is a form of sonic boom. It gives length and dimension to lightning, making the flashes more real and lasting in our memory. Yet thunder and lightning are so fundamentally different in character that only in the past couple of centuries did people suspect there was a causal relationship between the two.

At length, the storm passed to the east, as stately in its going as in its approach. The wind died first, the flashes grew fainter and fewer, and the thunder at last sank again into shapeless, flattened rumbles. Residual growls still came from the departing storm, like afterthoughts of violence thrown over its shoulder. Finally, all that was left was the steady patter of the binding rain.

July

The Fish That Wouldn't Die

Yesterday, I went dogfish fishing with my friend Ralph out of Sesuit Harbor in East Dennis. We baited our weighted hooks with leftover mackerel bits and threw them over the side. After twenty minutes or so, Ralph hooked a dogfish, a small, harmless member of the shark family. Only a few years ago, we would have cursed it and looked elsewhere for flounder, but now it was our primary prey. In fact, the small and slow-growing spiny dogfish has largely replaced the much-diminished cod in our inshore waters, and in recent years, it's become the basis of a multimillion-dollar industry. Despite its original abundance, however, the dogfish's slow and limited reproductive cycle, combined with the recent exponential increase in the numbers of dogfish harvested, have led to a estimated 80 percent decline in the number of mature females over the past decade. In other words, a species, only recently dismissed as trash, has become threatened almost before we've been able to get used to our change in attitude toward it from worthless to desirable.

In the next hour and a half, we hooked five good-sized dogfish, each about three feet long. Ralph flipped them into the boat, trying to avoid the long, sharp, venomous spines on their dorsal fins. As they thrashed about vigorously on the bottom of the boat, Ralph whacked each one on the skull with his knife handle in order, as he put it, "to slow them down." He even severed one fish's spinal cord at the base of its skull, but the fish continued to thrash about wildly. I had heard of the legendary tenacity of dogfish, but even this did not prepare me for what happened when we brought them back to my house to clean them.

Ralph set up a cutting table in the yard with two sawhorses and a piece of plywood. He drove a spike up through the bottom of the plywood and then impaled the head of each dogfish on the spike to hold it. As he cut into it, the impaled fish continued to move about. When Ralph skinned the first fillet and put it down, the fillet, too, continued to move, crawling slowly across the board. I must have looked startled, for Ralph commented dryly, "The difference between life and death in these creatures is argumentative."

But that was only the beginning of a bizarre display of persistence of life in these fish. Dogfish, like other sharks, are viviparous; that is, they give birth to live young. Nearly every shark we caught was a pregnant female, and each contained six or seven fully formed embryo dogfish. Some females actually began giving birth before we started cleaning them. Ralph speculated that this might be a "survival mechanism," releasing a "pod" of progeny in the face of imminent destruction. When he cut open the fish's oviduct, the embryos lay squirming on the board, their yellow egg sacs still attached.

We threw the embryos into the plastic gurry pail, where they continued to squirm along with the still-moving entrails. Later, we took the pail down to the shore and dumped the whole thing in the bay. From what we had witnessed, it seemed not implausible that the aborted fetal sharks might do just fine. Ralph, in fact, took two of the embryos home and put them in his aquarium, where they lived for several days.

Obviously, reasonable and expedient measures must be taken to manage and regulate this species, or it will soon go the way of the cod. Still, I confess I found it hard to be too sentimental or pessimistic over a life form that doesn't seem to know when to die.

Ant War

One peaceful, sunny morning earlier this month, I stepped out of the front door and into the middle of a violent war. It was an ant battle, and one of no mean proportions. The ground in front of me was thickly covered with hundreds of ants scurrying about in seemingly random motion. They were mostly small red ants about three-eighths-inch long. On closer look, I saw a number of larger black ants engaged in battle with some of the reds. Most of the other red ants were emerging from the ground carrying white, naked ant larvae in their mandibles.

This "war" covered nearly half the front yard, and I stood watching it in fascination for several minutes, trying to figure out what was going on. Knowing practically nothing about ants, I assumed that the red ant colony had been invaded by the blacks, who had gotten down into the red ants' nursery, causing panic and sending the reds into a massive rescue effort to move their young larvae to safety.

Two aspects of the battle, however, threw some doubt into this theory. First, if the blacks were the invaders, they seemed strangely nonaggressive. There were no pitched battles between individual black and red ants, only what seemed some harrying tactics by the reds. Moreover, the blacks made no attempt to take the larvae away from the red ants. The other thing was that the red ants carrying the larvae were retreating in a swath of organized columns five or six feet wide. I followed this swath of red ants across the yard where, carrying their white larvae burdens, they disappeared down into other ant mounds.

At this point, I decided to do some research, and after perusing several books on the subject, I found an explanation of the morning's events beginning to emerge that was much stranger than any of my ignorant surmises about ant warfare. War among ants is indeed a widespread phenomenon and has been chronicled since antiquity. (Thoreau describes an "epic" ant battle in *Walden*.) But even more common is the practice of ant slavery, and what I had been witnessing was likely a slave raid, not by the blacks, but by the reds. These black ants are relatively docile in nature and tolerate the more aggressive reds in their territories. From time to time, however, the red ants make coordinated invasions of the black ants' nurseries for the purpose of stealing their young. Strangely enough, the blacks offer little resistance, and, unlike true ant warfare, these slave raids rarely result in deaths on either side.

The black larvae are carried back to the nests of the red ants, where a number of them are eaten by the colony. But those that are allowed to hatch seem color-blind to their black heredity.

Like the legendary white-child captives of Indian raids, these abducted black ants live out their lives as accepted members of the red ant community, spending most of their lives helping to feed and harvest food for their captors.

So—I had exchanged my interpretation from "warfare" to "slavery," but where was I? A little closer to scientific accuracy, perhaps, but really no closer to the nature of the experience. How passive the victims seemed to be, how almost unaware of their invaders. Did the red ants feel "masterful," or the captive black ants "downtrodden"? Did they feel anything at all, in any remote human sense of the word? Could one imagine an ant abolitionist? No, they were still puzzles, red and black hieroglyphics of a summer saga, written in an ancient tongue I had neither the wit nor perception to read.

Vive la Différence!

Earlier this summer, Wellfleet increased its number of year-round food outlets by two. The two new businesses could not be more different. The first was PB's Boulangerie and Bistro, and it was a most improbable addition to our small town: a genuine French bakery and bistro, run by a pair of genuine French cooks, Philippe the chef and Boris the baker (the "P" and "B" of the business name). Both men left high-profile careers at hotels in Las Vegas to open a bakery-bistro business here.

Actually, the boulangerie opened last March, and at first, people thought it was a mischievous rumor. A year-round French bakery in South Wellfleet? What are they thinking? But the rumor was true, and from the beginning, there have been lines out the door waiting to buy fourteen different types of handmade breads, fruit tarts, brioche, meringues, macaroons, and many other delicacies. In late June, the bistro opened as well, and business has been thriving ever since.

PB's is located just off Route 6 in South Wellfleet on the site of the old Clam Shack. It's a lovely setting, beneath the shade of a magnificent oak tree fourteen feet in circumference with an herb garden at its base. The exquisitely decorated boulangerie, bistro, and expansive deck have quickly become one of the most popular—and crowded—gathering places in Wellfleet. We still don't quite believe it. As one friend put it, "I wake each day and say, am I dreaming? A real French bakery in our little town?"

The other new food venue, as I said, couldn't be more different. It's a Dunkin' Donuts, the town's first national-franchise store. It's located in one of the least attractive commercial sites in town: the old IGA mini-mall next to the post office on Route 6, fronted by a large, barren, cracked parking lot. Two previous local restaurants failed to make a go of it there. Dunkin' Donuts has re-paved the parking lot, but it's still a treeless sea of asphalt. The interior is—well—Dunkin' Donuts.

Predictably, the local response to the new Dunkin' Donuts has not been as welcoming as it was toward PB's. "Is that legal?" one shocked ac-quaintance asked when she heard of it. Another suggested a boycott, saying, "Perhaps we can drive them out of business." And another was afraid that it might be a threat to the new bou-langerie.

Unlike many of my friends, I have no prob-lem with the new Dunkin' Donuts. I doubt it presents any serious competition to PB's. Af-ter all, the two are at opposite ends of the coffee-cum-pastry spectrum. People who will drive thirty miles for a genuine French croissant aren't likely to be lured by mutant hybrids such as Boston cream donuts and bagel twists.

Nor do I think Dunkin' Donuts represents a significant threat to Wellfleet's "small town" self-image. For one thing, the location is so unattractive it will probably take a nationally known, reliable name like Dunkin' Donuts to lure people there. For another, it fills a community need, as there's no other year-round, sit-down coffee shop in town that opens by 6 a.m. Besides, I have seen other franchise stores become genuine local gathering places. It all depends on what they offer. Truth be told, their coffee isn't bad, and there are times when I'm in the mood for a glazed donut instead of a *tarte aux fruites*. In any case, it seems to me there's room, and business, for both places in our town—a place for both a real, handmade, flaky French croissant, and a real, mass-produced, predictable French cruller. *Vive la différence!*

Outer Beach Overnights

Over the past winter, I've been following the fate of the cottages on Chatham's North Beach. The new break in the barrier beach occurred during November of 2006 and has continued to widen. As it has, it has claimed more of the dwindling numbers of cottages that remain. I found myself feeling genuine sympathy for the owners of these cottages, some of which have been in the same family for generations. But I've also admired the way that most owners seem to be accepting the inevitable loss of these structures with philosophical resignation. In a way, these beach cottages represent the last waterfront structures on Cape Cod whose owners can *afford* to let them go without significant financial loss.

Still, I see them go with regret. I know the freedom from civilized discontent that these cottages celebrate, for I have something of a personal history with one of them. So I'd like to use this occasion to pay homage to them and add a couple of small stories to their legacy.

During my first summer on Cape Cod, I worked as a counselor at Camp Viking in South Orleans, one of a dozen or so sailing camps that once dotted the shores of Pleasant Bay. The camp owned one of the cottages on North Beach that was known as the Outer Beach Cabin. On occasion, a couple of counselors would take their cabin's campers in a whaleboat across the bay for one or two overnights in the Outer Beach Cabin. These trips were always sparked with a spirit of adventure and even mild lawlessness that would surely not be tolerated now. Distinctions between counselor and camper tended to break down out on the beach, and sometimes we aided the boys in the prohibited-but-universally-indulged-in nighttime activity of digging "beach-buggy traps."

A beach-buggy trap consisted of digging a deep hole on the beach in one of the existing beach-vehicle tracks that recreational fishermen followed when driving down the beach for night-time fishing. At dusk, we would dig the hole two- or three-feet deep, then hide behind a dune, waiting for the next pair of headlights to come bouncing down the beach from the north. We watched in anticipation until one of the head-lights suddenly dropped at an angle, signifying that we had "caught" a beach buggy in our trap. Then, we stifled our conspiratorial laughter as a stream of profanity issued from the invisible driver.

But the peak experience of my Outer Beach adventures, and one that secured me a small immortality in the legends of the Outer Beach Cabin, came during the summer of 1962. One day, Pete Ferreira and I took our cabin of boys, aged eight and nine, to the Outer Beach for an overnight. That evening, totally against all camp rules, Pete and I rigged a makeshift sail on the whaleboat from bed sheets and sailed several miles across the bay into Chatham Village. There, we took all of the boys to see Sean Connery and Ursula Andress in the first-ever James Bond movie, *Dr. No.* After the movie, we took them all for ice-cream cones and then sailed back to the Outer Beach Cabin. Of course, I'm appalled now at what we did, but whatever risk we took seemed insignificant in the light of the wide-eyed and unbelieving faces of those young boys as we sailed back across the bay under starlight. And though we swore them to secrecy about our adventure, I know that that moment still shines bright in many of their memories across the decades.

The Old Shell Game

This is about crows. Or rather, this is about *a* crow. I stress the singular, because if there's any lesson in the incident I'm about to relate, it's to caution us against generalizing about other animal species. We're all too quick to talk or write about "owls" or "woodcocks" or "whales," as though each one we encounter is totally representative of *all* owls, woodcocks, and whales, and that individuality is purely a human trait.

Anyway, the other day, I stepped out onto my front porch and was confronted by a large black crow that was perched on the porch light fixture. It was less than two feet from my head and peered down inquisitively into my face. If you've never been looked at down the nose, or beak, by a crow, I can tell you it's a somewhat unnerving experience. I say it was "large," though it was probably only average in size. But I'd never been this close to a crow "in the wild" before and was impressed with its appearance. The complete blackness of a crow at short range is startling. It has sleek, jet-black feathers, almost iridescent, that overlap like fish scales down its back and large, black feet with "nails" rather than claws. Most impressive of all is the thick, formidable, black beak.

The bird seemed absolutely unintimidated by

me. In fact, he exhibited a noteworthy aplomb, a sort of dignified curiosity. And so, I did what all humans do in the presence of wild animals that appear tame: I fed him. I offered him some Ry-Krisp crackers, which he took, and when I placed a bowl of water before him, he dunked the crackers in the bowl for several seconds to soften them and then happily devoured them.

I remembered reading that crows like shiny objects, so I held out a couple of new pennies. These he deftly snatched from my fingers and proceeded to bury them a little ways off. After this, I decided I'd really test him. I went into the kitchen and came back with three small cups. I put another penny under one of the cups and then mixed them up in the old shell-game fashion. The crow watched intently, and as soon as I removed my hands, he walked over and picked up the cups one by one, found the penny, and buried it as before. Now it's true he only found the penny on the second try, but I repeated the game, and each time he found the penny on the second try. Perhaps he didn't want to stretch my credulity too far.

I watched, fascinated, wondering what to make of it. Perhaps he was a tame crow, perhaps not. Crows are, after all, individuals by nature. Their cleverness is legendary, surpassing that of their human adversaries. It took us until 1972 to realize that we couldn't exterminate the crow, and so we declared him a "migratory songbird." Well, if you can't beat 'em, protect 'em.

At this point, a second crow appeared, landed on a nearby branch, and cawed sharply. The first crow stopped playing the shell game immediately, looked up, and without so much as a backward glance, flew off with the other crow up over the pitch pines and out of sight.

Someday, I may study crows—*Corvus brachyrhyncos*. Someday, I may even try to put this afternoon's encounter into some behavioral perspective or objective interpretation. But all I know now is that as this crow flew precipitously off with his companion, I felt snubbed. He had, it seems, only been slumming.

August

Family Fun

One August weekend, I had a visit from my son, Christopher, and his two older children, Anna and Henry, who live outside Philadelphia. Anna was ten and Henry seven, and I had the pleasure of introducing them to two of the Cape's iconic summer experiences: whale watching and a beach party.

Well, I'm not sure that either of them would describe the first one as a pleasure. I took them out on one of the Dolphin Fleet boats in Provincetown. The weather was iffy—overcast, with a stiff northeast breeze—and as we boarded the boat, it began to rain—hard. As we rounded Long Point and left the harbor, the rain let up, but the water became rougher, and the sixty-five-foot boat began pounding into the teeth of the wind and six- to eight-foot seas. At first, Henry and Anna found it a thrilling ride, and they were excited when we came upon a mother humpback whale and her calf lobtailing off the port bow. But in a short while, despite the Dramamine that had been handed out beforehand at the snack bar, many of the passengers, including my two grandchildren, began to get seasick, and Henry and Anna spent most of the rest of the trip slumped miserably against their father's side, oblivious to whales. Still, they weren't as miserable as several of the adult passengers, who stayed inside the cabin the whole time, hunched over plastic bags and groaning, "I paid forty-five dollars for *this*?"

I was afraid that the whale-watch trip would become one of those negative memories for the kids, but I hadn't counted on the resilience of the young. By the time the boat returned to the wharf, they were feeling much better. Henry announced that he was "92 percent recovered," and Anna was already recasting the experience as a narrative that she would tell, asking us, "Remember the guy who puked in his hat?" We walked down Commercial Street to find pizza and ice cream.

That evening, we had a beach fire at Cahoon Hollow with more family and friends. The weather seemed to be trying to make up for the rough morning. The day had calmed down, and a gibbous moon, trailed by Venus's bright glow, drifted in the southern sky. A bank of stationary clouds hung several miles offshore like a shelf in a department store. While some of us got the fire going, Christopher played with the kids in the surf and then clambered up the high sand slopes with them. As evening descended, I wired forks to lengths of pine wood that Anna and Henry used to roast hot dogs, and after that we made s'mores—Henry's first.

The trajectory of the day, which had started on a low note, ended on a high one. As we sat there, feeding the fire, watching the liquid rising flames, listening to the beat of the rising breakers, and telling stories, I reflected on the magic of a beach fire. You don't need much: a fire, a few hot dogs, some beer and soda, and people who like one another—the rest pretty much takes care of itself.

At about nine thirty, Christopher gathered the kids up, and I was pleased see that Anna was reluctant to leave the place I had made for them. "I want to see the fire die down and help to put it out," she said. Her father, running his fingers through her hair, assured her that there would be many more beach fires in her life. And she, with irrefutable ten-year-old logic, replied, "Yes, but not *now*!"

Hummingbird

Few things in the birding world give you as much bang for your buck as a hummingbird feeder. A few weeks ago, a friend from New York gave us such a feeder. It was an ovoid about the size of an ostrich egg, made of clear glass with a red-plastic, twist-on bottom. Following the instructions, I filled it with a boiled mixture of one-part sugar to four-parts water and hung it above the railing on our deck, near the trembling green leaflets and puffy pink blossoms of the mimosa tree.

Within days, two ruby-throated hummingbirds, both females, showed up, dutifully poking their long, thin, needle-like bills into the two slots at the bottom of the feeder, like eager consumers making withdrawals at an ATM machine. Though they were only a few feet away from where we sat having breakfast, they showed absolutely no fear of us. When they had temporarily sated themselves, they flitted away, sometimes hovering briefly over the mimosa flowers.

Hummingbirds are justly celebrated as physiological marvels for their iridescent, jewel-like color; for their ability to hover and fly backwards, even upside down, as if equipped with personal jetpacks; for possessing the fastest wing beats and heartbeats in the avian world; for the ability of a bird weighing no more than a postage stamp to migrate nonstop hundreds of miles across the Gulf of Mexico; and so on.

But for me, the most remarkable thing about hummingbirds is not their flying abilities or physical attributes, but rather the fact that they don't *act* as if they are small. They act as if they have no idea that they are the tiniest of birds. Everything about them suggests stature. They're poised, not anxious, assertive, not shy. One hears them before one sees them, an aggressive, purposeful hum like a tiny buzz bomb, but one that can stop on a dime and reverse direction in an instant. They chase off other hummingbirds with a kind of fierce animosity. I could swear that one day I saw one spit at another. They chase off chickadees and other birds more than twice their size. I think they would chase off a crow or a hawk if one showed up. What preys on hummingbirds, anyway?

Yet their manner and behavior is not that of the feisty bantam. Hummingbirds are not little Mickey Rooneys compensating for their diminutive size by bullying and braggadocio. Rather, they seem like creatures that live in their own world where they *are*, in fact, large, and that it's merely an accident that they materialize and move about in our world, an accident that has not affected their self-image at all.

As D. H. Lawrence put it in his poem "Humming-Bird," "We look at him through the wrong end of the long telescope of Time, / Luckily for us."

The Shorebirds of August

Out on the dry, gravelly sands, the shorebirds of August group themselves in small, tight flocks, sanderling with sanderling, plover with plover. They come in with the tide, pushed by a strong, hot, southwesterly wind that makes the waters of Cape Cod Bay heave and lift. Shorebirds are the Cape's midsummer fall spectacle. By August, when most of us are still looking forward to our summer vacations, the season has long been over for most of these long-distance migrants. Black-bellied and semipalmated plovers, whimbrels and dowitchers, godwits, turnstones, knots, dunlins, sanderlings, and sandpipers—all are northern, largely arctic nesters that have only a few short weeks in which to court, mate, lay eggs, and raise and fledge their chicks. Most shorebird chicks are ready to fly three weeks after hatching, and the adults leave shortly thereafter. Of the fourteen species of fall shorebird migrants that are listed as common or abundant on the Cape, thirteen arrive here in numbers in July. A few, such as the least sandpiper, show up in late June—all heading south.

The black-bellies, the largest of our plovers and one of the most abundant fall migrants, are in various stages of molt. Some still wear full, black velvet breasts and face masks; others are mottled, with a tattered, mange-like appearance. From the sands in front of me, a flock of ring-necks, or semipalmated plovers, bursts out of nowhere, a sudden, spontaneous beach generation. A pair of lesser yellowlegs flies up from the group of sanderlings, white rumps flashing like flickers', uttering their urgent *chu-chu-chu* calls. A short-billed dowitcher feeds quietly in the mud of a marsh pool, and beyond it, a pectoral sandpiper.

They are always beautiful and welcome, these late-summer migrants of our outer shores. And there is a kind of intellectual thrill knowing that a flock of sanderlings, probing calmly on the shore like backyard chickens, are merely pausing here on their way from Greenland to Chile. Their numbers are greater and more concentrated than in spring, but the autumnal spectacle tends to be a more subtle one. In the fall, the birds are muted in plumage and more casual in movement. Fall shorebirds, like fall warblers, are more difficult to identify than their spring counterparts. Moreover, although they show a greater variety in size than any other bird group, there's a compelling, underlying unity about them. Shorebirds share a strong common denominator of shape, sound, color, and movement that is born of a shared life of high, wind-hewn journeys and northern-tundra breeding grounds.

Yet though shorebird plumage, especially in autumn, shows very subtle variations, these differences are nonetheless remarkably fine-tuned to their habitats, even in migration. For instance, the piping plover (one of our few resident nesting shorebirds) has a pale-buff back and frequents the lighter-colored upper sandy beach, while its very close relative, the semipalmated plover, has a brown back and prefers the darker, lower, pebbled beaches and mudflats.

To know the shorebirds of August is to master the earth's subtleties. They shift and blend on the sands like a set of Bach inventions, subtle works of form and movement rather than of color and high romance, but all are products of the planet's deepest creative forces.

Mosquito

I'm being bitten by an insect. I came into this shaded beech grove to avoid the heat of the day; and now, as I sit here, cool and contained, a mosquito has found me and landed on my bare forearm. I sense her when she alights on my skin hairs, but I feel too lethargic even to brush her away. Moreover, I've never actually watched a mosquito bite me, and I realize that I'm curious to see exactly how she does it. (And yes, it is only the females that suck blood.)

For most of us, there's something repellant about letting an insect, or any creature, draw something out of you. I suppose it violates some deep sense of self, despite the fact that science has shown us that our bodies are inhabited by millions of bacteria and other foreign organisms, and that certain of our own cell components often behave like autonomous, genetically alien beings.

Still, it takes a sustained effort of will to allow the mosquito to position herself deliberately on my arm. She flexes and braces her hair-like legs in preparation; then the hair-thin, rapier-like sucking tube, or proboscis, pierces the skin and plunges into my flesh. I feel only the slightest pinprick of my nerve ends. As she sucks, the mosquito appears to bend down her head, so that the proboscis is bent somewhat back, perhaps to help lock it into place.

For a full minute, I watch her thin abdomen slowly swell dark and red with my own blood. The bite doesn't begin to itch until just moments before she withdraws her tube. Once this is done, she takes off immediately. The whole thing seems to have been timed perfectly to just avoid her victim's awareness. All that is left is a little, white, swollen lump on my arm with an invisible hole in the center.

Now, if I'd been mauled by a lion, or even stung by a bee, I'd certainly have strong thoughts about the matter. What then, is a mosquito bite to me? I realize that deliberately letting it occur at all, and observing it so analytically, is a geographical luxury. I happen to live in a malaria-free part of the world, and even the danger of the mosquito transmitting the eastern equine encephalitis virus is remotely small. So I can indulge my writerly curiosity fairly safely.

I don't begrudge this flying leech her blood meal, necessary as it is to her reproductive cycle. Rather, it's the *manner* of her feeding that I resent. If only she didn't possess that maddening, irritating buzz. If only she didn't tickle my arm hairs so stealthily, so insidiously. If only she could hone her rapier a little more finely so that I wouldn't feel it enter at all. And most of all, if only the anticoagulant she inserts before beginning to suck my blood didn't produce that annoying, persistent after-itch, which adds irritation to injury. Except for these things, I think I could live with mosquitoes as easily as I do my intestinal bacteria.

In fact, I recently read somewhere that some species of mosquitoes appear to have adapted to slapping by developing an anesthetic so that they can pierce the skin without the victim feeling it. But then, after twenty-five million years, I suspect the mosquito doesn't feel much obligation to evolve a more ingratiating means of violating our bodies.

September

Wednesday afternoon was one of those bright, sparkling, September days that we live for and just want to walk through all day long. It was a day that confirmed F. Scott Fitzgerald's assertion that life seems to begin anew when the air first turns crisp in the fall. My wife and I, with our dog Putt, went to the beach, following a path from one of the ponds through a cut in a small dune that had been worn by the innumerable feet of summer.

Just north of the cut was one of those improvised beach shacks that seem to spring up over the summer, made of driftwood and other available flotsam washed up on the beach. These impromptu shelters seem to have no more functional purpose than sand castles, but, like them, seem to spring from some atavistic architectural urge to create some structure at the edge of the land, to leave our signature on the beach.

This one was tucked into the base of the sand cliff. It was in the shape of a trestle, with two short posts connected by driftwood cross ties, sloping back into the cliff and creating a shallow lean-to shelter about ten feet wide, eight feet deep, and three and a half-feet high at the opening.

The roof was boarded over with driftwood two-by-fours, providing nearly solid shade, but hardly waterproof. The lintel post had been painted black, and on it, the word *Welcome* was printed in white letters. Flanking this word were several child-sized handprints in white, reminiscent of those handprints found in Paleolithic caves in France and Spain.

Despite its primitive structure, the bones of the shelter were highly furnished and decorated. The sides were covered in white canvas sheets, in which there were small holes charred around the edges. A lobster pot was placed at the back of the space, providing a low table or a shelf to lean against. There were two broken, aluminum-frame folding chairs inside. But the most impressive addition was a series of hangings nailed over the opening, most of them onion bags containing beach pebbles, shells, beach glass, and gull feathers. There was a lobster buoy and a rather large stone hanging from a rope, to which a green toothbrush had been attached. It seemed to have all the amenities.

We went inside the shelter and sat on the sand, and I was struck at how instantly this simple structure framed the ocean, as if we were watching it on a screen inside a derelict movie theater. Putt placed herself in a Sphinx-like position, crossing her front legs, directly in front of us, just beyond the nonexistent threshold, and all of a sudden, we became some kind of primeval family, looking out of our cave, as if we had always been here and always would be. It was as close as I have ever come to a racial memory.

There was an unexpected but powerful sense of peace and great groundedness that seemed embodied in Putt's utter look of animal contentment and belonging. "Who would need more than this?" she seemed to say.

Punks

We called them punks when I was a kid growing up outside Newark, New Jersey, in the 1950s.
They grew in the marshes that bordered the
Hackensack River. The marshes were frequently
on fire from oil spills, and in any case, they consisted mostly of phragmites, or reed grass: tall,
worthless, invasive plants that made the marshes
so barren that when convicts escaped from nearby jails into the vast labyrinth of the marshes,
the police wouldn't even bother to send their
dogs in to find them. They'd just wait a few days
for the convicts to stagger out weak from hun-
ger because nothing of any sustenance grew or
lived there.

But cattails, or punks, as we called them, grew
there, and in late summer, when the seed heads
had matured into those dark, cigar-shaped forms,
we'd cut dozens of them and try to wait until the
stalks turned all brown and we knew they were
ready. Then we'd light them and "smoke" them,
though we knew it was just pretend and no smoke
actually came up the stalk; and then later, when
we became teenagers and could really smoke if
we wanted to, we continued to smoke the punks,
saying they helped keep the mosquitoes away,
which maybe they did, but that wasn't the real
reason, and we knew that, too. It was just that

we had acquired a taste for the way they smelled. A lighted punk smells like the end of something and the beginning of something else, a bitter-sweet, nostalgic smell, even when we didn't have anything to be nostalgic about yet.

And so wherever I lived, I've looked for them and lighted them up in the fall, partly to remind me of my childhood, but mostly because I like the smell. It's the smell of fall. In most places, I get a kind of weird look from people when I walk by with a lighted cattail in my mouth. In other places, I've met people who also lit them as kids but did not "smoke" them. But never, anywhere, outside of northern New Jersey and metropolitan New York City, have I ever met anyone who called them punks. And when I do, it's like a secret handshake, or a distinctive accent; I know, without asking, that we share a common geographical and cultural background.

I call the kind of weather we've been having the past few weeks the punk-end of the season, because if you light one when it has dried enough to burn but the stalk is not completely dry, then, when the punk burns down to the last inch or so, the heat begins to send the remaining juices in the stem bubbling up into your mouth and the taste is as sweet as sex. So the punk-end of the season is kind of the distillation of every autumn you've ever known, and a punk-end day is like a late afternoon in early October when the air is soft and overcast and the ponds are flat as glass and some late-season swimmer wades bravely out into the water while his adolescent son remains on the shore like a dog, wildly throwing stones into the water and telling his father he's nuts, and you're walking with your own dog down a narrow path hung with Virginia creeper gone all red and eventually you turn into a road that passes by a couple of horses and you stop and they give you that look of surprising intelligence and then you go on and someone you love unexpectedly turns into the road and starts towards you. That's punks.

Crab Charity

It's not every day you get a lesson in crustaceans and charity from the same source. The other afternoon, returning from Hyannis by a back route, I came to a spot where the road crosses a tidal creek several miles inland. I got out to look around and noticed a young boy perched on some rocks where the channel comes out underneath the road. He was about ten or eleven, red-haired, and freckled. He was holding a dip net with a long handle and wearing rubber boots that were filled to the brim with water. As it turned out, though, his boots were not for keeping his feet dry.

"What are you fishing for?" I asked.

"Crabs," he replied, not taking his eyes off the water as it swept by.

"Blue crabs?'

"Yup."

At first I thought I'd encountered one of the last practitioners of the Cape Codders' fabled reticence, but suddenly, he swooped his net down into the murky waters and came up with a small, struggling blue crab about four-inches wide. The catch seemed to loosen his tongue.

"They start to swim through here when the current starts to flow in," he informed me. "It's all muddy and crapped up when it's going out, but it starts to clear up now, and you can see them swimming along on the bottom. You have to throw them back if they're less than five inches or there won't be any left, but this one I'm going to keep for my science class."

The boy gingerly began to transfer the crab from his net to the bucket, not an easy feat, for the crab's temper, to use an old pun, is snappish, and its appearance is no less intimidating. Armed with two strong front claws, the crab has a shell that's drawn out into a sharp point on each side. The front edge of it is also serrated like a rough knife. To remove one from a net is like poking your fingers into a snapping, clacking pincushion. The purpose of his boots became apparent.

"We used to catch them to sell," he went on, "but we only got fifty cents apiece for them, so I went into my own business, and I give them away to whoever comes along. You can have the next one I catch."

I thought this was a refreshing use to make of a poor market and hoped that local economic-development councils would be glad to hear of this public-spirited example of free enterprise.

Just then, some friends of his came canoeing through the culvert, and he went off to talk to them. I stood there admiring his ability, his sportsmanship, and especially his eelgrass-roots knowledge of life in this creek. It's the kind of firsthand knowledge that comes from just "messing around," and that no science class or textbook can teach. Here, I thought, begins the lifelong naturalist.

Then, in the clearing water, I saw what looked like a large crab clinging to a piece of seaweed in the current. I called the boy over, and he crept swiftly down the rocks, swung his net down, and hauled up not one but two good-sized, wriggling crabs. I could already taste the succulent crab meat for dinner, but the young philanthropist scrambled back up and raced over to his companions to show off his catch. Apparently, his recently formed Crustacean Foundation had been suddenly dissolved, and I realized that if I wanted crab charity, I'd have to begin at home.

Grassroots Movements, or Pea-Party Politics

We've heard a lot during this election season about grassroots movements to "take back our government." As with our use of most natural metaphors, we tend not to examine their literal meaning, in this case, "grassroots." I thought of this the other day when I walked out into my small garden, which I've neglected for the past several weeks. This is the time of year when gardeners, at least casual ones like me, start to abandon the daily tending, weeding, and harvesting of our crops. As the season winds down, our moral fiber grows lax, and we become more tolerant of alien weeds and insect pests, not to mention deer, raccoons, and groundhogs. Like an occupying army, we have largely abandoned an outlying territory we no longer need, at least until next spring, and in doing so, we find that native energies and residents have reasserted their claims.

In one unmulched corner of the garden, a number of tall, spike-leaved thistles have invaded the now-undefended perimeter. Their slender, five-foot stalks bear candelabras of white, hairy seed tufts, milkweed-like seeds that drift across the garden like a dry snowfall. They rise up through the pitch pine branches toward the white clouds and blue sky with that breath of adventure of all seasonal migrants in them.

Goldfinches visit the garden daily now for these seeds. They alight on the main stalks, then walk out on the side stems, curving and bending them down like Frost's country boys swinging birches, until they reach the seed tufts. There, they work at them industriously, if inefficiently. They shake them loose in scattered, fugitive bursts, sending ten aloft for every one they take, dispersing the seeds even as they harvest them. I once saw a female finch take off after a single escaping seed ball. After a few yards' chase, she snatched it on the wing like a nighthawk taking a moth.

Finches feeding on garden thistles are, I suppose, a common enough sight this time of year, but it underscored for me the many different functions that each organism, plant, and animal performs in nature. Who can say what the *main* function of any form of life is, what it is good for, or meant for, beyond perpetuating itself? For that matter, what are people good for? We should not feel guilty for the fact that we use the earth's resources to live. That's not only human nature, but the nature of all things. We have no monopoly on exploitation; all life is opportunist. We ourselves, our bodies, our homes, our crops, even our waste and pollution are all exploited by innumerable other organisms.

No, our error is in assuming that *our* use of any life form or resource is, in the language of property tax law, the "highest and best use," and that it therefore justifies our usurpation of all other uses. But in the face of nature's own manifest multiple-use policy, such an attitude is not only dangerous but constitutes a self-defeating presumptuousness. The horrific BP oil spill in the Gulf of Mexico is just another dramatic example that only through increasingly expensive, complicated, and risky resource-extraction systems can we maintain the illusion that the earth is inexhaustible and exists solely for our use. Nature insists on sharing the earth's resources with all of her creatures, and by doing so, she puts democracy to the acid test. Perhaps that's why Americans have remained for so long insensitive to her basic principles. But just look at an abandoned garden, and you'll see how, when one group gets too powerful, nature *will* take back her government.

October

Wood Ducks

One morning recently, as I sat at the table before the glass doors writing up some notes, I looked up and saw a group of wood ducks—three males and two females—perched on an oak branch at the edge of the yard less than sixty feet from where I sat. Now I've seen wood ducks all my grown life, but I've never gotten used to seeing them in trees. I know it's natural for them—after all, a preference for woodlands is where they get their name—but it hardly seems sensible. Seeing a duck in a tree is like seeing an owl swimming in a pond or a turkey soaring high overhead in the clouds.

Still, one doesn't question wood ducks when one gets them, wherever they are. I would welcome one in my mailbox—and that's not as far-fetched as it sounds, given that they prefer to nest in mailbox-size hollows in trees. In New England, the wood duck is also known as the summer duck, because its wintering grounds are largely below the Mason-Dixon Line. And unlike most local ducks, it won't take to coastal waters when hard freezes close its freshwater haunts. Thus, on the Cape and Islands, it's considered, as one source puts it, "a casual winter straggler, surviving only if fed artificially." Hmm—seems like that could apply to me as well.

But wood ducks *are* startlingly beautiful. Other ducks—mergansers and teal, for instance—have just as many square inches of bright color as the wood duck, but they don't begin to approach it in beauty. The male wood duck's vivid plumage is concentrated in its iridescent-green head and light-blue primary wing feathers, a red-orange bill, and a bright-red eye. But its body is dramatically set off with flashy streaks of stage white that heighten the contrasting plumage and give the bird a strange ritualistic appearance, like some stock character in an avian *commedia dell'arte*. The plumage of the female, as is commonly the case in the bird world, is less showy and more subdued than the male's, but it's distinguished by a broad, white eye ring.

Their tree-perching habit is just one more extraordinary thing about these birds. As the five wood ducks sat there, arranged boy-girl-boy-girl-boy, I expected them at any moment to start singing or to spout poetry. Lined up on the oak limb, framed so close to me in the glass doors, they didn't look like real birds—or rather, they looked more than real. I felt that wood ducks should not be walking around in the real world at all, but set upon some golden bough in a glass museum display case, "in a lifelike attitude."

Well, so much for impressionism. These ducks were real enough, and all the better for being so in a Cape Cod oak tree. For five minutes they sat there, like squat tropical parrots, the males occasionally dipping their emerald heads up and down to no one in particular. And then, as if to disabuse me of my too-aesthetic appreciation of them, one of the females defecated as she took off and flew directly over the house. Then she swooped back down towards the kettle hole bog, drawing the other four off with her. They threaded themselves expertly through the dense maze of gray limbs and bronzing leaves and were quickly lost to sight. I felt at once suddenly bereft and deeply blessed.

The Bridge to Nowhere

Last week, I took a walk along a wood road that borders the Herring River. A few hundred feet in, there's an old, narrow, rickety wooden bridge that crosses the stream. When, why, and by whom it was first built, I have no idea. Possibly, it was originally constructed by duck or rabbit hunters to give them access to the marsh on the far side of the river, though hunters seem to have largely abandoned the area.

In any case, when I first moved to town, the bridge was already in a dilapidated state and seemed about to fall into the river. And yet, someone always seems to make jury-rigged repairs to it just before it does. In fact, since I was last here earlier in the summer, unseen hands had nailed weathered eight-foot, two-by-twelve boards on top of the rickety, rotten planks below and had rigged a cotton clothesline as a token handrail along the downstream side.

What I find strange about these periodic ongoing repairs is that the bridge seems to be a bridge to nowhere. That is, once you do get to the other side, there's no trail, no path, no obvious direction, only a nearly impenetrable tangle of catbriar that keeps you from advancing any further. The bridge now seems to be repaired purely for its own sake, merely, like the

147

proverbial chicken, to let you get to the other side.

And so I did. I made my way across the twenty-foot-wide stream, holding onto the clothesline as I went. At the far side, I sat down on the bridge planks, resting my feet on the bank, facing upstream with the declining autumnal sun at my back. I pulled a punk - a dried cattail - out of my pack and lit it, savoring the deep, musky odor of the blue smoke that curled from its brown tip. It was a warm, still, collected afternoon. The stream before me was covered by a green mat of floating duckweed, with spears of green leaves rising out of the mat, tinted in gold. It was all a gold-and-green scene, with no obvious autumn colors, more like a Rousseau painting of still, tropical lushness.

As I sat on the bridge above the slowly moving water, something changed. I became aware that I had "latched" onto the scene. There was no epiphany, no apparition or revelation. But I experienced a change of perception and pace as definite as a key turning in a lock. There seemed to be a slow smoothness and softness to everything around me, muffling both movement and sound. The only evident motion was that of the narrow, black stream, silently carrying its waters under the bridge toward the sea. A breeze, gentle but perceptible, made only the softest, quietest rustling in the leaves. The wings of a bluejay, coming in for a landing on the branch above me, made two or three soft flutters as it perched that I would never have heard in any other situation. A single pinecone falling from the high branch of a pitch pine into the duff of the forest floor sounded violently plosive, like a soft bomb. In the air, a large black-and-white dragonfly glittered like a lacy-winged skeleton. The smoke from the tip of the punk that I held in my mouth slowly uncurled and wafted upward above the stream. It circled and skated in the air, giving form to the almost imperceptible breeze. Time closed down and held us in a timeless moment. That was all, and yet I thought, what else do we live for?

Occasionally, I get a query from a listener who asks me, "Just where is it that you live?" Well, as I've explained before, I generally keep the locations I write about deliberately vague, not just for privacy's sake, but so that others can discover similar things in their own locations. As someone once said, if you can't find Walden in your own backyard, you'll never find it.

Nonetheless, I thought today I'd try to describe where I live in a way that best expresses its essence, if not its exact location. And the phrase I've come up with is "between two worlds." I mean that both literally and figuratively. Let me explain:

On one side of our house is what used to be known as the town dump. Well, actually, it's still called "the dump" by just about everybody except town officials. Over the years, its function and name have gone through an evolution common to just about every town on the Cape and Islands. The town dump was, for decades, just that—an open dump, where town residents brought their garbage, trash, and demolition materials and heaped it on a growing pile of debris. This was either burned or informally covered over with dirt.

Later it became a "sanitary landfill," which

is a euphemism, or an oxymoron, I'm not sure which. Anyway, residents still brought their garbage and trash there, but open burning was no longer allowed, and state regulations required that trash and garbage had to be covered with an impervious layer of clay. It was also about this time that a recycling program was started at the dump, taking newspapers, glass, plastic, metals, and bottles.

Then, several years ago, the Commonwealth mandated that all local landfills had to be closed, capped with nonporous material and rubber sheeting, and surrounded by a chain-link fence. The dump was now officially renamed a "transfer station," and garbage and trash was, in fact, trucked in huge steel containers to an off-Cape incinerator and burned.

But it's still a dump—that is, we still take our garbage and trash and refuse and dump it there. It's just disposed of elsewhere, a system that won't bear too-close environmental examination.

For over twenty years now, our dump, like most towns', has had a swap shop, a place where people can drop off items they no longer need or want and that, theoretically, still work. The swap shop building actually used to be the house of our current fire chief, Danny Silverman. He donated it to the town when he got married and built a new one. The swap shop is a technological museum of sorts, full of recently or not-so-recently obsolete items such as typewriters, dot-matrix printers, LP records, cassettes, VHS tapes, laser discs, even an occasional eight-track tape. But it also contains a plethora of useful items—wine glasses, lamp shades, window blinds, etc. We've furnished a significant part of our house from the swap shop, including a four-poster maple bedstead, a 1930s art deco stained-glass lamp, and a brilliantly painted Guatemalan liquor cart, just to mention a few of the choicer items.

On the other side of our house is a very different world, the world of the Cape Cod National Seashore. Technically, our property actually touches the boundary of the Seashore at a vanishing point at the far end of our lot. But it's enough to make us feel connected to it in a special way. What it means is that we can walk out our door and into over a thousand acres of preserved woodland, moor, freshwater swamp, salt marshes, rivers, and beach—having to cross a road only once and usually without seeing more than one or two other walkers, even in summer. The reason is that this section of the National Seashore has no signs telling anyone that something is there.

Unlike such official Seashore attractions as Coast Guard Beach, the Marconi Site, the Red Maple and White Cedar Swamps, Highland Light, and Race Point, the attractions of our portion of the National Seashore are not posted in signs or labeled on any maps. In fact, before the Seashore was established in 1961, much of this area was known locally as the *outback*, a term I've always liked. *Outback* has connotations of lawlessness. It suggests an undefined, unnamed, unmanaged, and informal wilderness. Every town used to have its outback, an area outside the settled centers of town where people went to get wood or hunt or picnic or engage in unsupervised adolescent adventures or romantic trysts, or just wander around. Most towns have lost their outbacks over the past fifty years due to the intense development on the Cape and Islands, but we are one of the fortunate ones that have had our outback officially preserved, but without officially defining or labeling it.

Now, I'm not as lucky as those fortunate few who actually live in "inholdings," that is, houses that are within the boundaries of the National Seashore. But that's okay. I'm not sure I'd want to be that privileged. The burden of appreciation might be too much. It's enough for me that my land touches, however marginally, such an environmental buffer. I can dip into it on a daily basis, renew my acquaintance with its familiar but ever-changing features, or be surprised by the unexpected—such as a peacock on the bridge over the Herring River, or a treasure trove of morel mushrooms under a low-growing grove of oaks, or an albino fox.

So, that's where I live: on one side of my house, the town dump; on the other, the National Seashore. One a place for the refuse of civilization, the other a refuge from civilization. Both are places of give and take. To the one, I give my trash and recyclables, and take used but serviceable items. From the other, I take solitude, inspiration, and the healing sense of something larger than my own needs and desires, and give back, I hope, some words that might help others to hear its voice.

It's not a bad place to live, balanced between two such worlds.

Flounder Fishing

On the last afternoon of October, during a sweet stretch of balmy weather, I set off in my skiff with a couple-of-dozen night crawlers to spend a few hours flounder fishing on the calm and clear waters of Nauset Harbor. Anchoring off a sandy point, I throw in two sets of baited hooks and wait for signs of gratitude from below. When fish are biting well, there's usually not much time for anything but hauling in line, unhooking fish, and resetting. But the run of the tide is beginning to slow and the flounder with it, so that I have time to jiggle my tarred lines between thumb and fingers before pulling them up.

Even without such a practical justification at the other end of your line, Nauset Harbor is a wonderful place to spend an Indian summer afternoon. A few lobster boats ride placidly at anchor. Hundreds of pots are heaped in mounds on the lower part of the beach. Partially submerged in the rising tide, they look like skeletal reefs, rising menacingly out of the water. A cormorant fishes in the shallows, diving with little fillips and emerging again.

To the east, the long, white arm of Nauset Spit stretches northward longingly and empty. At its far end, I can just make out some turbulence in the water, indicating the Inlet, the channel entrance from the ocean, and beyond that, the truncated arm of Coast Guard Beach. To the northwest, the bare, grassy crown of Fort Hill lies shining in the October sun.

I seem to see the encircling scene more clearly than I do in summer, partly because the low sun lends contrast and shading to each feature, so that shapes resonate rather than blend. I realize, with something of a start, that relative to the winter solstice, this afternoon is the equivalent of late February. How the tides of the season lag here, casting lengthening shades of reluctance and regret over all endings and partings.

It's a lovely and a peculiarly empty day, as I sit in my small boat, jigging my flounder rigs in the clear, green waters. Not only are the summer crowds missing, but many other recent noises and sights as well. Gone are the screaming clouds of common and least terns that nested all summer on the sandy plains of Nauset Spit and on the grass-covered dunes of New Island. Gone, too, are most of the shorebirds of late summer and early fall. Only a few black-bellied plovers, a lingering yellowlegs or two, and flocks of bright sanderlings forage on the disappearing flats and along the tidal wrack. The migrating swallows that cruised the spartina prairies and the wandering monarch butterflies that straggled down the beaches in late September have all flown.

On the other hand, the large flocks of eiders

that regularly feed on the estuary's mussel beds have not yet arrived, nor has the herd of young harbor seals that spends the winter months fishing its waters and hauling out on the frigid beaches and islands of the harbor.

It's a slack time of year, a time between seasons and currents of life, between the growth of more salt marsh behind the dunes and the attrition of the Outer Beach in the face of winter storms. Like the flounder that I *assume* are hooked, waiting to be pulled up and turned into fish dinners, the year seems to be lying quietly at the bottom, waiting for some sea change.

November

Intelligent Design

The local term *scratching*, like *clamming*, is sometimes used to refer to any kind of gathering of
shellfish with a pronged instrument. But used
properly, *scratching* refers only to the harvesting
of quahogs, or hard-shelled clams, with a quahog
rake. As such, scratching is a highly accurate and
descriptive term. Soft-shell and razor clams can
lie a foot or more below the mud of the tidal flats
and must be "dug" out with a clam rake, a short-
handled tool with thick, bent tines. Scallops lie on
the surface and are more properly "raked" with
an instrument very much like a garden rake with
a basket attached. Oysters, of course, can simply
be picked up off the flats by hand. But quahogs
generally lie *just below* the surface of the flats and
are therefore "scratched out" with a quahog rake.

Scratching for quahogs is in itself a highly satisfying activity. Although it superficially resembles
hoeing or cultivating, it's a slower, more careful
work, something like pulling loose teeth from
soft, rotten gums. In early November, I love to
set myself against an outrunning tide, eelgrass
streaming before me, and methodically rake my
rows across the sandy bottom. The curved rust-
ed tines of the rake give a soft shush with each
sweep through the sand, as I wait for the feel
and sound of the hard, rocky scratch that signals

a buried quahog. The lines made in the muddy sand remind me of the pronged chalk holders used by my grade-school music teachers to draw wavy music staves across the blackboard. My own moving prongs strike and reveal the buried quahog, which sings its sharp squeal against the metal tines.

A well-made quahog rake is one of those nearly perfect tools, superbly fitted to both use and user. A properly made rake stands slightly over four-and-a-half-feet tall and has an ash handle tapering slightly down its length. It thickens again where it enters the metal socket. The six steel tines that protrude from it are curved and vertically flattened so that they slip strongly, yet smoothly, through the mud and sand. The tines are just long enough to reach the maximum depth to which a quahog will burrow itself, and they are spaced widely enough so that anything smaller than a legal-sized quahog will fall through.

A quahog rake is not only perfectly designed for its primary function, but it is also admirably suited for a variety of other manual tasks at other times of the year. In spring, I use it to rake salt hay off the beach for garden mulch; in summer, I dig potatoes out of their hills with it; in fall, I use it to pluck apples for cider out of roadside trees. It's also the most effective tool I know for clearing out thickets of the dreaded catbriar.

Its long handle allows me to stay out of harm's way from the catbriar's thorns. The wide, curved tines will hook the vines and pull them out, yard after barbed yard, and yet easily disengage from the tangle once I've dumped the vines on the brush fire. Talk about intelligent design! No other tool I know of is so at home and of such varied use at all seasons, on both land and sea, as the humble, sturdy, and versatile quahog rake.

November Woods

I'm not sure what it is about November days that makes them so likely to bring on fits of melancholy and somber moods, but they do. Maybe it's the final bareness that emerges behind the glory of the fall, the skull behind the mask. Maybe it's just the prevalence of clouds and the tightening ring of cold around the diminishing warmth of the days. Whatever it is, when soul and weather match in mood, there's nothing to do but give into it at once, to track the mood down to its source and purge it through indulgence.

So, late one warm, misty afternoon last week, I took myself to a piece of woods I'd not walked before. I knew the road where it began and the marsh where it came out a halfmile or so beyond, but not what lay between, except that it looked sufficiently somber for the day and me.

The woods began with stands of open pitch pines, remarkably clear of any underbrush. This had evidently been a pasture and was crisscrossed with well-made stone walls. The walls were still in good repair, thanks to the lack of heaving frosts on Cape Cod. The pine needles lay everywhere like a mat, soft and yellow brown. It seemed it could not have been that long ago when cows wandered slowly across this gentle slope and gazed with incurious wonder at the distant sea.

Further toward the marsh, the land began to drop off more rapidly into a series of small ravines and steep slopes. Here, falling prey to gravity, the stone walls had come undone and were tumbled down, like lines of truncated meaning. Near these fallen remnants of the walls were several groups of larger boulders, two and three feet across, which had apparently been deliberately placed together there. Near them, the sockets of earth from which they had been plucked by men and oxen were still visible. For what purpose had they been arranged like this? Who knows—who can remember now?

Most of the boulders were thickly covered and half-concealed under a layer of pine needles. They peered out at me from under shaggy brows. Here, the woods lay thicker, and darkness was beginning to fall like a fine net. Overhead, the chopping sound of a helicopter drew near, then faded. Across the valley boomed the guns of November, blasting away at quail and pheasant in some unposted woods.

The temptations in such scenes are far from philanthropic, but I was here to give into temptation. What I loved about the scene was the sense of oldness and desertion. It seemed that no one had been in these woods for a hundred years. Only the boulders, like presences, brooded under the thick silence of yellowed pitch pine needles. I got on my knees and dug away the coating of needles and loam from one of the stones. There I found a rock surface of pink granite, unusually bright in color, like a bird's egg. The surface was very rough but clean, perhaps from having been eaten into by the acid of the decaying pine needles. It seemed incalculably ancient.

There, in the gathering darkness, I felt that I might stay and become, like the rock, immensely old. Gradually, I, too, would be covered with the detritus of living, harboring only a pink spark of consciousness. At last, I would perceive only faintly the muffled din of thunderstorms and the wind down the valley, and not at all the self-willed movements of men on wings and wheels.

The green wall of summer is dismantling itself. After the extended clemency of this unusually warm autumn, the oak leaves are finally falling in small flocks or in mass migrations earthward. And as they fall, the sliders and the glass windows on the south walls of the house begin to let in not only late-autumn sunshine and a greater sense of exposure, but a totally new dimension, even a sense of unreality, to what happens inside.

The effect can be powerful, illuminating our own mortality or those of others. One late-fall afternoon several years ago, my father stopped to visit. He sat with his back to the glass doors, the sun low behind him. As we talked quietly over coffee, my eyes slowly adjusted to the brilliant sunlight behind him, so that his figure seemed to darken, lose detail, and become a shrunken silhouette. His body became a mere cutout against the consuming glare of the sky and the cryptic pattern of the shimmering tree branches behind him. I had a sudden, overwhelming sense that he was disappearing before my eyes and felt a painful urge to reach out and draw him back. Instead, I consciously averted my eyes and offered him more coffee.

At this season, dusk is the most powerful time of day. At supper, I sit at one end of the table facing the large glass windows to the southwest. The sun has just set clear, and the myriad interlaced branches of the oaks grow first dark, then black against the dying light. Then, perspective itself goes: The thin oak limbs cut and weave across one another in a flat plane like a thousand shears, snipping apart the plaited continuities of the day. It's a stark sunset ballet, at once full of terror and peace, as though seen down the long, destroying corridors of the centuries.

If it's not too cold outside, we leave the shades up throughout the evening. As night comes on, the black glass panels finally begin to give us back to ourselves. They show us our reflected images gathered around the lamp at the table, as in so many dark mirrors. Our reflected shapes are somewhat blurred because of the double panes, and this effect plus the darkness give the reflections a kind of distance, as though we see ourselves on a stage, as if we are people whom we know quite well, whose futures we care about, yet whom we are somehow unable ever to tell what we know about their destinies.

It is at such times as this, I think, that we come as close as we ever do to imagining ourselves as we really are, reflected darkly out of the enclosing night. To see ourselves thus confutes our sense of a human-dominated world and throws us back into huddled pinpoints of light and vague, ominous glows against the horizon. It is for this that

I love the night. It gives a return of perspective, dissolving the bounded blue sky of day into a universe of lights rushing away from one another into endless folds of space.

The Secret of Life

In an essay entitled "The Secret of Life," Loren Eiseley wrote that he considered autumn the best time of year for pursuing that elusive notion. Others, he knew, preferred the rising juices and the bubbling noises of spring, but, as he put it, "I have come to suspect that the mystery [of life] may just as well be solved in a carved and intricate seed case out of which the life has flown, as in the seed itself."

I don't usually walk in autumn with such a lofty purpose in mind, but November is certainly the best time for discovering some of the small secrets of life, if not the Secret itself. One of these small secrets, so cleverly hidden all summer, is the location of bird nests, which are themselves a kind of seed case out of which the life has literally flown. In November, the abandoned nests have not yet been torn to pieces by winter storms. They emerge to our sight in the crotches of trees like old, hairy coconuts or else dangle from the stripped branches like small dance purses carelessly flung up into some tree after the party was over.

Most nests, however, are not built so high up. If we get off the roads and begin to walk through the bleached fields and leafless woods, we find all sorts of evidence of hidden summer life: the wide, bulky nests of catbirds, usually placed in dense catbriar or virburnum thickets; the more delicate, cup-shaped nests of song sparrows, constructed entirely of grasses or tough rootlets and set low in bushes or cedar branches; the common grackle or robin nests, told by their middle layer of mud sandwiched between leaves and grasses and frequently found close to houses in blue spruces and other ornamental evergreens.

If you're really lucky, you may happen upon the exquisite, diminutive cup of the goldfinch, a jewel among nests. It's composed of fine grasses lined with thistledown and carefully placed in the fork of a young sapling. The abandoned finch's nest looks extremely fragile, but it's so tightly woven that it's been known to hold the water of summer storms and drown the chicks within.

Two things about bird nests always surprise me. The first is how obvious they are once the leaves go, so that I wonder how I could have missed seeing them before. One yellow warbler has nested for three straight summers now on the same site along the road not far from our house. Its nests have all been built only a foot or two into the leaves of the scrub oaks lining the shoulder. Each November, the little grassy nest suddenly appears in the branches as if by magic. Each time, I mark the spot and determine to find the next one in spring. And each May, it eludes me again.

The other thing that strikes me about these deserted nests is how sturdily so many of them are built. Although most birds build new nests each year, many of them are made much better than they seem to need to be. It's as if the birds took a pride in their craft in building them that went beyond mere utility. Some I've observed have lasted longer than the birds that built them, before finally disintegrating under the elements.

In any case, these modest secrets of life can be found by anyone this time of year, right under our noses.

December

Incense of the Season

Late last Sunday afternoon, I walked out to Wing Island, a small marsh island in West Brewster. Wing Island is locally famous as the site of the first house built in the town of Brewster, around 1656 by the Reverend John Wing. No one knows exactly why he picked such an isolated spot in which to settle, although the abundance of salt marshes (which were used as early pastures) around the island was a likely draw. In any case, it would have afforded him and his family a secure, if somewhat lonely, home site.

I walked across the earthen dike, bucket in hand, to pick some of the island's plentiful bayberries to make into Christmas gift candles. Bayberries, of course, are the source of the celebrated bayberry candles and bayberry soap that are sold in many of our local gift shops. Bayberry grows in most places east of the Appalachians from Nova Scotia to North Carolina, but like its shoreline associate, the beach plum, it seems to thrive best in sandy soil within sound of the surf. It is the plant's bluish-gray berries that are the source of candle wax. They grow in small, tight clusters and in the fall become coated with small, waxy tubercles.

I found a thick patch of berries just off the main trail and began to pick them, rubbing them off the twigs between my palms or stripping them with a milking motion. As the berries fell like hard raindrops into my bucket, it occurred to me that Mistress Deborah Wing and her children very likely also picked bayberries on this same ground some three-and-a-half centuries ago. Probably she did not have Christmas candles in mind, though, since the celebration of that holiday was forbidden in early Puritan households, especially those of the clergy.

The virtues of bayberry candles were celebrated quite early. In his 1705 *History of Virginia*, Robert Beverly noted that "[bayberries] make candles, which are never greasy to the touch and do not melt with lying in the hottest weather: neither does the snuff of these ever offend the sense like that of a tallow candle, but instead of being disagreeable if an accident puts the candle out, it yields a pleasant fragrance to all who are in the room, insomuch that nice people often put them out on purpose to have the scent of expiring snuff."

The wax is obtained by boiling the berries in a large pot for an hour or two. The greenish-yellow wax melts and floats on the surface in large, transparent globules that are skimmed off after it cools. The candles can be made by remelting the wax in a narrow glass jar set in hot water and repeatedly dipping a wick into it.

I stayed, picking berries on the island until darkness began to settle, and then rose on stiff knees and headed back across the dike. I picked about two quarts of fruit, which are now bubbling away on the wood stove. If I'm lucky, I may get one four-inch candle out of my efforts. However, like the wood you cut yourself that warms you twice, bayberry wax smells twice, once when you're making the candles, and again when you burn them. Already, the house is filled with its soft, pungent fragrance, and on Christmas Eve, we will light a single, pure bayberry candle in homage to the ghosts of John and Deborah Wing, a small continuity that, I hope, might bind us a little closer to this gentle land of multifarious small pleasures. And perhaps, like one of old Beverly's "nice people," we, too, will snuff it occasionally on purpose to enjoy more thoroughly this sweet incense of the season.

Letting in the Sun

During the weeks approaching the winter solstice, I've been cutting down some of the pitch pines to the south of our house to let in a bit more of the winter sun. Overall, I've taken down about a dozen trees, ranging from about six inches to over a foot in diameter. I never do this lightly or without mixed feelings, balancing the trees' and my own competing claims. This is especially true here, on the site where I have lived now for barely over a dozen years. Virtually all of the trees on my lot were here before I was. This hasn't stopped me from cutting them, but it has given me pause.

When I cut down a tree, I usually count the rings on it, just out of curiosity to see how old it is, or was. With pitch pines, you have to do this in the first day or two after cutting, or the cut stump will glaze over with oozing pitch, like gray-white sugar icing on a coffee cake. When I counted the rings on one of the largest trees, well over a foot thick, I was struck to find that the tree was exactly my age. I counted again, just to be sure. Yes, it was my arboreal twin, sprouting in this place from a seed during the same year that I first saw light on the banks of the Passaic River in New Jersey over six decades ago.

When I examined the rings more closely, I even found a rough correlation between the periods of greater and lesser growth in our lives. After the first tentative year or two of existence, we both went through a growth spurt of about sixteen years to full-grown adolescence. There then followed, in the tree, a dozen or so years of reduced growth, perhaps reflecting a period of drought. My own life, in those years, was searching for a definite direction, full of false starts, doubts, and indecision. Then, at about age thirty, the tree took off again, adding twice as much sapwood in the next ten years or so as it had done in the previous dozen. During that decade I, too, put down permanent roots here on the Cape and began what has turned out to be my life's work. Unaware of one another, we each bent to our most productive years in tandem.

After that, our growth patterns diverged somewhat, with the tree settling down to more modest and consistent growth, as if reflecting a sureness about its place in the world, content to grow steadily if undramatically. My own life went through another series of upheavals, changes, and moves before coming to my present home. Here, I have settled down once again, as if drawing a certain stability from the pillar-like trunks of these trees with which I now share a common space.

It occurred to me that if I had been careless in my cutting, the tree might have taken *my* life. Instead, I took its life in exchange for a little more light, a little more warmth in my own. It would be nice to say that I gave thanks to the spirit of the tree for sacrificing itself for my use, but I didn't. That would have been a false appropriation of an older, indigenous ethos and ritual that I can appreciate, perhaps even try to emulate, but which I cannot claim for my own. But I do feel that I owe something to that tree, and its fellow pines, even if it's only these few words.

A Home of the Heart

Yesterday afternoon, I went to Cliff Pond in Brewster's Nickerson State Park. My intention was to see what winter ducks might be on the pond, but as it turned out, I found much more.

It was a misty, mizzling day, contracting the appearance of the earth and giving the woods a rich, formal aspect. There were a few-dozen black ducks and mergansers out near the middle of the pond. As I watched them, a large, dark bird flew out of the tall white pines above me. A crow, I thought, and at first dismissed it as such. Then its size struck me; it was much larger than any crow, or even a raven, for that matter. Then I saw the mottled white patches, the large, hooked head, like a weight, and the slow, deep wingbeats.

It was an immature bald eagle, the first I'd seen this winter. Its flight was leisurely and stately as it drifted across the pond toward the western cove and into the pines on the hills above it. I followed it with my field glasses, but at last, it disappeared in mottled splendor against the dark boughs and wind and rain. It seemed to be beckoning to me.

I walked along the shore to the western cove. It's a long, deeply indented cove, and at its far end is a small, grassy pond that was once connected to the larger pond but is now separated from it by a sandy isthmus that has built up over the years. Steep, pine-covered hills flank both sides of the cove, and the wind, which blew from the southwest elsewhere, was here twisted around so that it blew from the north straight down the gullet of the cove. The pebble-worn shores were lined with large, opaque slabs of ice, stranded like white fish. The rocks in the water were ringed with smaller, clear arcs of ice that one could pick up and view the world through in a distorted fashion. The inner cove was covered with a very thin but continuous layer of dark ice. It rippled in the wind with a strange, sibilant, seething crackle, a sound I have never heard ice make before.

I stood and looked out across the ice of the cove at the wind, the mist, the crisscrossing of squadrons of ducks, the gargling laughs and clean falling cries of the gulls. I looked across the open water to the far, obscured shoreline. And as I did, the cove took on an archetypal, enchanted aspect, like something encountered in dreams. It seemed like one of those homes of the heart that we sometimes suddenly recognize, a place that we have somehow always yearned for without knowing it, like Yeats's Isle of Innisfree or Thoreau's Walden Pond. Where these homes of the imagination come from it's hard to say. They may have some deep, ancient, mythic, even evolutionary origin, or they may have been engendered by some cheap romantic novel or movie we read or watched in adolescence. It doesn't really matter. We all know how noble, mortal passions can be brought out in men and women by the most trivial or unworthy objects. For me, I felt I could have built a small lake house there in that cove and remained for a long age, listening to the ice in its strange, new tongue, learning what it had to say—it seemed to have so much to say.

The Advent Whale

It was five years ago this week that a humpback whale washed up just south of Newcomb Hollow beach in Wellfleet. She was a six-year-old, forty-foot female named Beacon. We knew this because she had been named and followed for years by the Provincetown Center for Coastal Studies. Because she came ashore in the weeks before Christmas, some of the locals dubbed her "The Christmas Whale," or "The Advent Whale."

I first saw the body three days after it beached. By that time, the weekend crowds had dispersed, and there were only a few other curious onlookers. The whale lay near the base of the cliffs, draped over the break in the beach and oriented seaward, its massive fins splayed out on the sands. On its left side, the carcass had been cut or ripped open, and all of the guts had spilled out. Nearly all of the blubber on that side had been flensed, or stripped off the torso. Things were pretty ripe downwind.

At first, I didn't understand why the torso had been so thoroughly flensed, but I later learned that the Seashore would not allow the Marine Mammal Stranding Network to remove the carcass whole. They felt it was too environmentally risky to allow trucks or front-end loaders on the narrow, steep winter beach. So perhaps the flensing was a way of removing what they could to hasten decomposition.

I went out again the next morning in the midst of a driving northeast snow squall. This time, I had the whale to myself. The wind was herding green breakers onto the beach, and white snakes of snow dust hissed and sizzled around my ankles. When I came to the whale, the snow had cast a thin, white veil over its wind-ward side, as if trying to provide some shreds of dignity to its violated body. A small flock of gulls stood patiently on the beach a little to the south. I went around to the leeward side of the body, where its immense bulk provided a windbreak. The frozen air had stifled the stench as well. Sand had already begun to pile up on this side as well, covering one of the flippers. Perhaps, I thought, the beach would accomplish its own burial.

Far to the south, obscured in the flying snow, I saw a four-footed figure skulking along the base of the cliffs. When I lifted my binoculars to my eyes, it had disappeared. A coyote? A fox? A feral dog? We were not the only ones with an interest in this event or, for that matter, not even the ones with the most compelling interest. After all, it was just a whale to us, not a matter of life and death.

The day after Christmas, the whale was gone. A howling gale the night before seemed to have done the trick. I spoke to a man who had been on the beach during the storm. He said he watched the shelf on which the whale lay being under-cut by the surf, until suddenly the decomposing carcass rolled down the beach into the foaming surf and was gone. Just like that. The ocean had solved the cetacean-disposal problem on its own. It made the whale's appearance seem more like an apparition than an advent. There was no sign of it left on the beach or any sign that it had ever been there. Had it actually been there? The beach has a way of making even the most solid and permanent objects seem like illusions.

One evening this month, shortly after the ponds froze, I was having dinner with some friends. A young man named Caleb was there and mentioned that he had spent several hours that afternoon skating on Horseleech Pond. The frozen surface, he said, was "all black ice" and so clear that he could see lost fishing lures on the bottom twenty feet below him. Caleb said he enjoyed it so much that was thinking of going back out there later that night, when the moon would be almost full. Whether he did or not, I suddenly knew that I would have to see such a sight for myself.

So at ten thirty, I pulled into the small parking area beside the pond and walked out onto its frozen surface. The moon, one day past full, was nearly at its zenith overhead, hanging like a mirrored globe over a ballroom. Caleb was right. The pond was a perfect sheet of ice, as smooth and clear as a polished dance floor. If I had simply come upon it unawares, I would probably have thought that it was calm open water and would never have thought of venturing out onto it.

Walking out onto the ice gave me the strange feeling of walking out onto a great, glass-topped coffee table. Even by moonlight, I could see the bottom clearly at depths of several yards. I walked over miniature green forests of bottom growth that were absolutely still and sealed, a world under glass. As I got further out toward the center of the pond, though, I could no longer see the bottom. The only marks on the surface, except for a few stress cracks, were some wide-spaced skate-blade scratches, no doubt those made by Caleb earlier in the day. Remarkably, as I walked across it, the ice made not the slightest sound, not even when I jumped on it. There were no whoops or cracks of protest from the ice, just a perfect, frozen, silent pond.

Nor were there any sounds coming from the shore—no wind in the trees, no courting owls, though this is their time of year to woo. There was only the soft, distant, muffled beating of the ocean surf beyond the great hill of dune separating the pond from the beach.

I went running and sliding across the pond, into the northern cove where a pair of summer cottages sat along the shore, their windows dark and silent. They seemed like presences there in the full, stark moonlight, as if dreaming of the vanished summer life they held.

And then, as I started back across the pond, I saw something totally unexpected on the bottom: my shadow. Unlike most shadows, this one was clearly separated from me, detached and independent there on the floor of the pond.

I was seized by a sudden impulse to dance

with it, and so we twirled and glided across the ice, together but detached, my black doppelganger and I, in a synchronized ballet around the perfect rim of the pond, as the white moon revolved slowly overhead above the dark, illuminated waters.